Planting Mission-Sl

Planting Mission-Shaped Churches Today

MARTIN ROBINSON

MONARCH
BOOKS

Oxford, UK & Grand Rapids, Michigan, USA

Copyright © Martin Robinson 2006.
The right of Martin Robinson to be identified
as author of this work has been asserted by him in
accordance with the Copyright, Designs
and Patents Act 1988.

All rights reserved.
No part of this publication may be reproduced or
transmitted in any form or by any means, electronic,
or mechanical, including photocopy, recording or any
information storage and retrieval system, without
permission in writing from the publisher.

First published in the UK in 2006 by Monarch Books
(a publishing imprint of Lion Hudson plc),
Mayfield House, 256 Banbury Road, Oxford OX2 7DH
Tel: +44 (0)1865 302750   Fax: +44 (0)1865 302757
Email: monarch@lionhudson.com
www.lionhudson.com

Distributed by:
UK: Marston Book Services Ltd, PO Box 269,
Abingdon, Oxon OX14 4YN;
USA: Kregel Publications, PO Box 2607,
Grand Rapids, Michigan 49501.

ISBN-13: 978-1-85424-728-5 (UK)
ISBN-10: 1-85424-728-X (UK)
ISBN-13: 978-0-8254-6103-3 USA)
ISBN-10: 0-8254-6103-0 (USA)

Unless otherwise stated, Scripture quotations are
taken from the Holy Bible, New International Version,
© 1973, 1978, 1984 by the International Bible Society.
Used by permission of Hodder & Stoughton Ltd.
All rights reserved.

British Library Cataloguing Data
A catalogue record for this book is available
from the British Library.

Printed in Great Britain

Contents

Preface   7

Chapter One	Living between Paradigms	11
Chapter Two	The Changing Shape of Church	33
Chapter Three	The Art of Church Planting	49
Chapter Four	The Gathering Process	67
Chapter Five	Building the Team	85
Chapter Six	Discipleship and the Creation of Community	103
Chapter Seven	The Spiritual Life	123
Chapter Eight	Churches that Plant Churches	141
Chapter Nine	Simple Church	157
Chapter Ten	Going Public	173

Bibliography   191

Preface
How this book works and what it is intended to do

These few words are important in that they will help you to access the book that follows. Some have asked me, why are you writing a book on church planting, surely enough books already exist? There are two answers to that question. First, as I surveyed the number of books on church planting, I found far fewer than I had expected. I have included an annotated bibliography (p.191) of the most important books on church planting that I am aware of. As the bibliography makes clear, each of these books serves a different purpose and all have a place of value on the bookshelf of the church planter or mission strategist.

Secondly, I originally wrote a book on church planting called *Planting Tomorrow's Churches Today* with my co-author Stuart Christine. That book was written between 1990 and 1991 and published in time for a major church planting congress in Britain in 1992. That book is now out of print and the original request was to revise the book substantially so that it could be republished. As I reviewed the book I came to realize that it was not really possible to revise the book as it stood. I was surprised at how much has changed since the book was written. My major criticism of the book is that it is too mechanistic in style. It seems to suggest that there is a fixed process or method that one can employ which leads to a successful church plant. There is much in that original book that is valuable and so I have decided to make it available as a free download from www.togetherinmission.org or from www.martinrobinson.com.

It seems to me that it is now necessary to think in much less mechanistic terms and much more in organic terms when considering the issue of church planting. As the title suggests, this book attempts to connect thinking about church planting with a wider debate about the nature of missional church, with discussion about the nature of leadership and with a debate about the relationship between church planting and movement. I am working with the assumption that tomorrow's church planters will want to be participants in a movement of mission rather than be agents of evangelistic enterprise alone, valuable as that may be.

What qualifications do I have to talk about church planting? I was born in 1950, the eldest son of a church planter in Bihar, India. My father was greatly influenced at that time by his friend and colleague Donald McGavran, founder of the Church Growth movement. After my father's return to the UK, he became a church planter, first in Scotland and then in England. My first experience of ministry as a clergyperson was with a small inner-city congregation that had to be treated effectively as a re-plant situation. That small congregation went on to plant directly or indirectly a number of other congregations.

I eventually went on to lead one of those church plants at the same time as operating as the General Secretary for the denomination of which I was a member. Our strategy as a denomination at that time was to church plant as fast as we reasonably could. Apart from my personal involvement in a church plant, I have acted as an advisor to other church plants, written training materials on the topic and worked closely with the British inter-church agency for church planting, Challenge 2000, now called Together in Mission (TiM). I am presently the National Director of TiM.

My original intention in this book was to provide an updated comprehensive handbook for church planters that took account of the new situation of postmodernity. I am no longer convinced that it is possible to write such a book. I say this with great care because I am aware that some other books exist that attempt to do just that and I want to commend the authors for their efforts. I would also suggest that you buy those books but apply them with a degree of care because the situation of the West is sufficiently complex that even if we begin with the advice of an expert, in the end we will need to find our own highly contextualized answers.

This book therefore attempts two very different tasks. The first is to begin a conversation with church planters, all of us seeking to learn from each other in a highly complex situation of mission in the Western world. The second is to open a conversation that attempts to hold in creative tension three elements. The first element is that of understanding the complex context in which we are attempting to church plant. The second element is to highlight some practical issues for church planters in the context of the theme of missional DNA, and the third element is to think through how church planting relates to the question of movements.

The book is organized to reflect these three concerns. The first two chapters pick up the broader contextual issues. The next five chapters (3 to 7) attempt to address some practical issues that church planters must face as they attempt the planting process. These issues are presented as the basis for discussion rather than as fixed answers or even recommendations for action. The following two chapters (8 and 9) address the question of church planting and the generation of movements, and the final chapter attempts to bring all three of these issues together as a conclusion.

In the writing of this book I owe a special debt to the following people. In relation to the debate in chapter one on the DAWN initiative, Gerald Coates, Bob Hopkins, David Coffey, Lynne Green and Roger Whitehead have all offered clarifications and corrections that have been very valuable. In relation to the chapters on team and spirituality, I am grateful to my colleagues Tony Sands and Roy Searle who have written extensively on these subjects for the MA in Missional Leadership that Together in Mission has helped to produce. Their work is reflected in these chapters.

As this book will make clear, I believe the following – that the West is in need of a process of re-evangelization sufficiently deep that the whole of its culture needs to be renewed. I am convinced that church planting will play a part in that process. I am as sure as I can be that the church that emerges from this process will look very different from the church we have inherited and that few can guess what that shape will be. The process of re-evangelizing the West will not be easy, it will take at least one generation and possibly more, but it is possible to accomplish.

The external signs are not hopeful, the demographics of our situation in the West look discouraging but God has in mind an open future, one that is not yet decided. We dare not be complacent but neither should we be defeatist. The questions that many in the West are asking are profoundly spiritual in nature. We must not fail our compatriots in the West by lacking the spiritual energy to engage with those heartfelt questions.

Chapter One
Living between Paradigms

A few months ago I was sitting in the attractive suburbs of Sydney with a group of church planters. In true Australian style, the barbeque was hot and the evening full of lively banter leading eventually to some intense conversation. My new acquaintances wanted to know if they could ask me a few questions. The list was long and it nearly always began with 'How do you ... ?' There was nothing wrong with any of these questions and indeed they must be asked, but it is not the question set with which this book begins.

What we might call 'how' questions are often asked by practitioners, in this case practitioners in church planting. How do we understand our community, how do we gather the first group of believers, how do we evangelize unbelievers, how do we research our community, how do we reach across cultures, how do we reach young people? These and many other 'how questions' are entirely valid and they are always the primary issues when we are living in a fixed and familiar paradigm. When that is not the case then to begin with 'how' questions is to court disaster.

As virtually every philosopher and social commentator would agree, the Western world is currently living between paradigms. The shorthand that we use to understand the current cultural shift is to talk of modernity and post-modernity. In very simplistic terms, the worldview, or cultural underpinning of the West for the previous three to four hundred years has been that of modernity. That settled worldview has come under serious challenge over the last thirty years from philosophers who have suggested that we are now in a postmodern phase. Although there is widespread agreement about the foundations and shape of modernity, there is as yet no such agreement as to how to describe postmodernity. Critically, there is not even agreement as to whether postmodernity forms the basis of a new worldview or whether it is merely a critique of modernity, clearing the ground for a worldview which is yet to emerge.[1] What we can agree on is that modernity has not entirely faded from the scene and yet it seems to be fatally wounded. At the same time, postmodernity is itself in a process of transition and change. The new paradigm has not arrived, the old is surely dying – we are truly living between paradigms and that is not a comfortable place to be.

The experience of living between paradigms is not a new one for the church. The church in the West, and particularly in Western Europe, has experienced such radical transition before. Think, for example, of the period AD 500–600 when the relatively settled church of the late Roman Empire had to come to terms with the invasions of predominately pagan peoples. These invasions dramatically changed the economic, social, political and cultural landscape. The church that emerged from these societal convulsions looked significantly different to the church that initially encountered them. Indeed there were many who wondered if the church would survive at all.

In similar fashion, the church that eventually emerged from the traumas of the religious wars and societal conflict of the sixteenth and seventeenth centuries (the Reformation and its aftermath) looked very different from the church that had existed before this period. The issue for the church in these periods of change was not so much about the 'how' of survival but about the deeper 'what' that related to the very nature of the church. The church had to recover its missionary heart, and the consequence of that process was to produce very different manifestations of the church.

Mission always seeks to contextualize the gospel in relation to the culture that it seeks to address. That is not a difficult concept when we are thinking of the preparation of missionaries who are going to be sent to other lands. Of course they will need to know the language, the worldview, the customs, the assumptions and the religious outlook of those they are trying to reach. The gospel will need to assume appropriate 'clothes' for the new setting.

We are not nearly so practised at engaging in a similar act of preparation for a Western setting. Neither should we be surprised. The approach of the church to a Western world set in modernity has been familiar and, until recent years, relatively successful, at least in terms of winning a place of recognition and respect for the utilitarian value of the church in society. Having said this, we might be less confident about the success of Christianity in modernity to win a place for the gospel in terms of ultimate truth claims. But whatever the successes of Christianity in relating to modernity, finding a way to relate to the new and emerging culture of postmodernity is both more difficult and potentially more exciting.

At such a time, it is necessary to re-examine the structure of mission that we have inherited and to look, not just at the building but at the foundations as well. In other words, before we can ask the 'how' questions, we need to ask the 'what' questions. In particular, what is the essence of Christianity, what is the church, what is the gospel, what is mission, what is evangelism, what do we mean by church planting, what kind of churches should we be planting, what is leadership and what do we mean by ministry?

It is not the purpose of this book to explore all of these questions, though I will offer some working hypotheses in relation to some of these questions and address more specifically the questions relating to church planting, leadership and ministry. For the moment I want to suggest that Christianity is at its best when it operates as a lay movement and spreads its message most effectively when it is structured to support the initiatives of lay people. That does not mean that there is no place for clergy but only that their primary purpose is to equip and empower lay people for mission. In that context, the church is what happens when the followers of Jesus meet together to engage purposefully in mission. For the purposes of this book I intend to use the five marks of mission as a working definition of mission.[2] With that definition in mind I am suggesting that evangelism as a living expression of the message of Christianity, that is to say, lived and spoken, is a legitimate part of mission though not the whole of mission.

There are those who protest whenever the 'what' questions are addressed. The orientation of the activist (and sometimes the missional activist) is such that he or she sometimes has little patience with 'what' questions. They want to get on with mission. They see the urgency of the task and can tend to see any reflection on 'what' questions as an unhelpful and unnecessary diversion of energy from mission. I have a certain sympathy with this position in that I have met those rare and imaginative individuals who are so tirelessly and creatively wrestling with the 'how' questions that they intuitively address the 'what' questions without even realizing that they are doing so. These individuals are that rare breed of missionaries who, by nature, are already experimenting with the church that will emerge.

As I have indicated, these are the exceptions. The majority of us will need to take at least some time to think through these 'what' questions precisely because the answers to these issues critically impact and shape the 'how' of our actions. I am not suggesting that we do nothing in the meantime. It is vital that we engage in mission even as we address these questions and this book is written in the fervent hope that many will be planting churches, but as we do so we need to ensure that these uncomfortable 'what' questions are deeply impregnated in our hearts and minds. Our provisional answers will need to be tested in the mission field, not merely considered in the library.

The shape of the West

This book is written in the hope that it will be useful to practitioners across the Western world. It is therefore important to ask whether we can speak about the West as a single entity. What do we mean when we speak about the Western world?

Traditionally, the West has been imagined as Europe (and more recently Western Europe) and its offspring in terms of population, culture, economics, technology, media, political systems and common Christian heritage. In terms of geography we are describing Europe (both East and West), America (both North and South), Australasia and to some extent parts of the world which though not traditionally part of the West are significantly incorporated into Western institutions, such as Japan, and possibly in the future, nations such as Singapore and South Korea.

But is it useful to think in such terms when it comes to producing a book on church planting? Is it not the case that these various parts of the West are so diverse that each region would need its own very different book? There are clearly huge differences between the cultures of North and South America and even between Canada and the United States of America. Western Europe is very different from Eastern Europe and the northern part of Western Europe very different from the southern part. We could go further. In terms of religious history and experience, the Czech Republic is vastly different from its neighbour Poland, France from Italy and Romania from Hungary. Even at a national level the situation of the church in Oslo is remarkably different from the church in the south-west of Norway, and Perth's response to mission is somewhat different from that of a practitioner in Melbourne.

Certainly there are huge differences between nations and indeed continents across the Western world, but there is one common cultural phenomenon that has impacted much, though not all, of the West. As we have already indicated, the West is living between paradigms and that single fact influences all of us in the way we do church. For much of the West, late modernity has sought to marginalize the church, to exclude it from the shaping of the future, to expel it from the public square, and to privatize it in such a way as to emasculate its vigour.[3] For many, Christianity has become the past that the West is seeking to escape and not the future that it aspires to. We could describe the forces that have impacted Christianity in this way as a kind of secular fundamentalism, intolerant and at times deeply irrational. Its manifestation and effects have been very different in the various nations of the West, but the same themes are ever present – notably the cry for freedom, represented always as an objection to constraint of any kind.

More seriously the impact of secular fundamentalism and the undermining of the Christian vision that gave birth to modernity threatens to destabilize the whole of Western culture. As one writer has suggested:

> What exactly is Western civilization, and what holds it together? Politicians, asked to define what we are fighting for in the war 'against terrorism', will always say freedom. But, taken by itself, freedom means the emancipation from constraints, including those constraints which might be needed if a civilization is to endure. If *all* that Western civilization offers is freedom, then it is a civilization bent on its own destruction.[4]

Yet despite this twist present in late modernity, the shift of paradigms so worrying for some in the church precisely because of its rejection of modernity, contains within it the possibility of a new and much more encouraging horizon. Consider, for a moment, some extracts from two newspaper articles both published in British newspapers within a few weeks of each other.

The first is written in a broadly left of centre serious newspaper and reflects the kind of attitude of late modernity that most of us in the Western church have experienced on many occasions. The refusal to regard faith of any kind with any degree of seriousness characterizes this attitude.

> Religious belief is now almost never seriously discussed among the kind of people I know and the same is true, I suspect, for most readers of this newspaper. Religion as sociology, religion as ethnicity, religion as politics and ethics, relgion as art, ritual or good works, religion as the best route to a good C of E [Church of England] primary school: we can and do talk about these. But religion as faith and as an explanation of the world – why God exists, what happens after we die, who gets to heaven (or hell): most of us would run a mile from such a conversation. We know that the argument was won long ago and there is no point in discussing it. Real believers (as opposed to the soppy 'there must be something out there' brigade) are infrequently encountered and are not in any case amenable to what we believe is reason. They have their private beliefs let them get on with it.[5]

The second piece is also written in a broadsheet newspaper, this time a slightly right of centre newspaper, by someone who is not a Christian but who carries considerable respect as a commentator on issues that relate to science and religion. This second writer begins to offer another perspective which points to potential future attitudes.

The first point to be clear about is that British secularism tends to blind us to reality. This last Christian cult – for that is what, at heart, it is – is based on a myth. This myth is that religion is just what people did before they had science to explain the world to them.

The cult of secularism has, from a global perspective failed miserably...

All of which is to say that the truth, to which the British have been blinded by their contemporary myth, is that there really is only one beleaguered and threatened faith in the world today and that is secularism

This puts us, as minority believers in this minority myth, in a very odd position. We can still say, of course, as many do, that we are the future, that the process whereby scientific reason conquers religious faith is still in its infancy and that, in time, the world will succumb to our rationality...

We may even say that the progress of liberal democracy will be the political leading edge of this process. The problem is that there is absolutely no evidence that this is happening; in fact all the available evidence is that it is not. Advancing secularism as the creed of the future is a statement, of pure faith, a wishful-thinking elevation of our own local cult to global significance...

For 'secular' Britain this means our self-defined ideology of disobedience is both highly aberrant and, in human terms, impossible to maintain. The secular belief in progress, in the future, which was intended to supplant religion, has failed...

There has to be a starting point, a home. And ours is, on this Easter Sunday, as on every other, Christian Britain.[6]

The thoughtful realization that secularism as a belief system has its limits and that faith, in particular the Christian faith, has a contribution to make is one of many glimmers of hope beginning to emerge in the new landscape that we have so far called postmodernity. The potential friendliness of postmodernity to a new and faith-filled way of shaping tomorrow is beginning to dawn on a number of writers, not least some evangelical thinkers. The shape of the West is by no means fixed and Christians can help to shape its future.

A British contribution

Despite the hope that this book will be useful in many Western contexts, the fact remains that it is undeniably written from a British perspective. That may indeed be an advantage for the following reasons. The connections between North America and Britain remain significant and potent. For better or worse, many evangelical British Christians look to the American church for inspiration and encouragement. One only has to see attendance at events as diverse as Willow Creek conferences, Purpose Driven Church conferences and even Emerging Church conferences, let alone to earlier influences of Peter Wagner, John Wimber, and many others to realize that the transatlantic currents run strong and deep and usually in one direction only. (The Alpha course is one notable exception to this tendency.) But curiously, some of the American experience, especially in places such as the north-west and the north-east, with their teeming immigrant populations, feels more like Britain than they look like the boomer churches in the heartland of evangelicalism in the Midwest. The same is true among many of the young postmoderns across America. It is just possible that the British experience of decline in the church accompanied by a history of a much greater degree of hostility from the public square might have some lessons which can be of value in the USA. At the very least, the American church can receive a graphic account of what might happen to it if some significant changes are not made.

Despite the proximity of Canada to the United States and despite the tendency of Australians to look increasingly to the United States for leadership and to weaken the older ties with Britain, there is much in both these societies that feels more like Britain than the United States. Solutions and insights forged in these lands are likely to be of more mutual value than mono-cultural imports from the United States.

In very different ways, Britain, however reluctantly part of Europe, does share a common European culture, which in some important respects allows lessons painfully lived in Britain to have some currency across Europe. Although the experience of decline may not be as severe as in some European churches, still the British church has experienced huge numerical losses. The failure to include any reference in the proposed European constitution to a common Christian heritage was a shared European indicator of the weakness of the church across Europe. In addition, unlike the United States, Canada and Australia, most parts of Britain do have some experience of a state church with all the advantages and disadvantages that such an arrangement brings.

For all these reasons, the British church, in trouble but not yet in despair, weak but still with some significant resources, may be able to serve as a kind of missionary laboratory from which others may learn. Church planting has been and is being attempted in Britain to a degree that allows some observation to take place. In particular, there was an attempt in the 1990s to engage in saturation church planting using the DAWN strategy. In the view of a good number of observers, this attempt was both a failure and for a number of reasons, a misguided experiment.

Enough time has now elapsed to revisit this experience and to offer some comment. It is essential that we make some assessment because, in Britain at least, the supposed failure of the DAWN experiment represents an immediate reason to exclude church planting from the agenda. The experience involved such a large segment of the British church that it is almost impossible to speak further about church planting (except as a kind of marginal activity that has to be tolerated but the less of it the better) without some appraisal of this initiative.

The DAWN movement and the experience of saturation church planting

In the late 1980s it was apparent to a number of observers that something new was taking place in the area of church planting. Of course, some church planting had always occurred but in the 1980s the normal experience of church planting seemed to take on a new intentional significance. It was coming to be regarded as a mission strategy and not just as a means of meeting particular and unusual needs in new housing areas. There were a number of tributaries contributing to this fresh stream.

Anglican Church Planting Initiatives (ACPI) was begun as a ministry by Bob and Mary Hopkins in 1987 in the town of St Helen's, Lancashire. Their initial success gave rise to a number of largely Anglican conferences held at Holy Trinity Church, Brompton. The attendance at these events, several hundred strong, not only included Anglican evangelicals but Anglicans from a number other traditions and notably, a few attendees from other denominations. It was at this point that this began to feel like something more than a point of interest and something more like a movement.

At the same time that ACPI was developing, the organization Oasis, which was founded by Steve Chalke, a Baptist minister, began to offer one-year mission placements and training for young people in a variety of British contexts, very often in inner-city situations. The Frontline Teams, as they were called, caused the issue of church planting to be raised with the particular outcome that the Baptist training college, Spurgeon's, agreed to offer, in partnership with Oasis, a three-year course intended to train church planters. The existence of a potential stream of trained church planters clearly raised the issue of church planting for Baptists. Since that time the work of Stuart Murray-Williams, initially at Spurgeon's and then with Urban Expression, has been significant among Baptists.

A similar organization to that of Oasis, begun by Rob Frost and working mainly with the Methodist Church, developed Seed Teams some of which began to work in existing churches engaging in mission and a few of which gave attention to church planting. In these relatively small ways, church planting had been raised as an issue in the three largest Protestant denominations in Britain.

ACPI operating in St Helen's had been greatly helped by Youth with a Mission (YWAM), and church planting was an issue that had occupied the attention of this organization. It was difficult for them to begin to plant YWAM churches because they were a parachurch agency and had no intention of becoming a denomination. Nevertheless the leadership saw the strategic importance of church planting. It had entered their radar screen as a mission issue. This was particularly so for the UK director of YWAM, Lynne Green.

A leader who had worked closely with Lynne Green of YWAM, Roger Forster, was busy pioneering new models of church planting in south-east London under the umbrella name, Ichthus. Their work had begun in the 1970s but by the middle 1980s was coming to the attention of a wider audience. Not only had this organization planted 'strawberry runner' congregations in London but they were also training young people on an international basis and encouraging church planting in many nations as well as in various parts of the UK. At this time Ichthus looked and felt more like a church planting movement than merely a church planting local church.

A number of the new church networks, notably, Pioneer, Harvestime and New Frontiers, were also vigorously planting new congregations. The leader of Pioneer, Gerald Coates, had co-operated with Lynne Green of YWAM and with Roger Forster of Ichthus in developing a number of mission initiatives, notably the March for Jesus events, during this same period. These functions and relationships began to include Sandy Millar, the new Rector of Holy Trinity Brompton which was already hosting the ACPI conferences and had pioneered one particular model of planting.

While these relationships were developing, a different but related group of evangelical leaders met regularly for conversations at the Atheneum Club in London to discuss a range of issues that impacted mission, their organizations and the Christian scene in Britain. The late Roy Pointer, who was then the Director of Church Training at the British and Foreign Bible Society, was one of these leaders. The issue of church planting arose in this context and it was suggested that the Bible Society might call a consultation on church planting to test whether there was a new movement developing. Roy agreed and gave the task of calling the consultation to his Church Growth Consultant who at that time was this author.

The consultation took place at High Leigh, Hoddesdon, in February 1991 and was jointly sponsored by Bible Society, the Evangelical Alliance and March for Jesus. Approximately seventy church leaders came from some twenty different denominations. In total they represented all of the major denominations and networks together with most of the smaller denominations in Britain. Just before the consultation took place, Roger Forster and Lynne Green had attended an event in Singapore which had profiled the work of the DAWN movement in the Philippines. As they heard this strategy outlined they began to wonder if this was exactly the catalyst that was needed to propel the incipient church planting movement that they were aware of towards becoming an instrument for the re-evangelization of Britain.

The DAWN strategy was given a major hearing at the

church planting consultation. It transpired that a good deal of work had taken place before the consultation and it was suggested that a new interdenominational agency be launched. The suggested name was Challenge 2000 (with the millennium in mind) and a logo which had already been prepared was presented for approval. It felt to some as if the consultation had been hijacked by the three DAWN enthusiasts. However, it would be wrong to suggest that anyone was concerned by this. On the contrary, there seemed to be a widespread enthusiasm for the proposals as presented and indeed a degree of gratitude that someone had engaged in some work prior to the event such that there was a concrete outcome as compared with yet another consultation statement.

Following the High Leigh event, a charity was quickly established, a full-time worker to lead the new organization, Chris Forster (the son of Roger and Faith Forster) was recruited, and the DAWN strategy began to be implemented. An integral part of the strategy was the holding of a number of DAWN Congresses. The suggestion was that these would be held every three years to galvanize support, develop strategy and review progress towards the stated goals.

The first of these DAWN Congresses was held at the Birmingham Christian Centre, in the centre of Birmingham, in February 1992. Around 600 church leaders attended and once again, virtually every denomination and stream in the UK was present. At this event, a goal of planting 20,000 new congregations by the year 2000 was adopted. From a promotional point of view this made good headline copy. However, there were a number of significant problems that flowed from the adoption of this goal.

First, the process of arriving at the goal was somewhat flawed. There is some disagreement about the exact composition of the process. The figure of 20,000 is significant in that the original DAWN process in the Philippines suggests the goal of one evangelical church for every barrio (an administrative district composing around 1,000 people). Transferring that goal to the UK would mean approximately 60,000 churches for a population of just under 60 million people. Since research suggested that there were just under 40,000 congregations already in existence that would mean it would require 20,000 churches to complete the task.

The dispute concerns the extent to which the figure of 20,000 churches as a desired end goal was already in the arena for discussion before the goal was set. The process was to arrange for the different denominational groups to meet in their respective conclaves and to agree the goal that each would take responsibility for. When these were added together they came to 20,000. A remarkable co-incidence, a Spirit-led result or projections driven by an awareness of the desired outcome? That is the area of dispute.

Second, those who were setting the goals usually (though not always) had little or no capacity for committing their respective denomination to the stated goal. These individuals were often enthusiasts for church planting rather than representatives of their denominations. They might agitate for the adoption of a given goal but they could not guarantee its acceptance. Having said this, the enthusiasm that they represented did act as a spur to action.

Third, little thought had been given to the question as to whether a strategy that had proved effective in a developing nation which was receptive to the gospel as it was being presented by Protestant denominations in a largely nominal Catholic nation would also be effective in an unreceptive developed nation. The method was presented as the effective ingredient. The issue of contextualization had not been faced.

Fourth, the process in the Philippines involved setting a goal for the year 2000, in 1974, giving a time span for completion of some twenty-six years. This represented the national church owning a task for something like a generation, whereas in England the taking of the same end point of 2000 gave less than ten years and seemed to be driven by unreasonable focus on the millennium or unrealistic hope of revival.

Fifth, those who were familiar with the Philippines DAWN strategy were aware that there were at least two elements which were crucial to its success in the Philippines which were either ignored or at least were not developed in the British context. The most significant of these was the widespread development of evangelistic home Bible study groups. These were the critical cells, which, when brought together, would form a grass roots church planting movement. No provision for introducing an equivalent structure was made.

Sixth, few of those at the Congress had access to resources that would enable goals as extensive as these to be accomplished. The level of infrastructure, especially in terms of leadership training, still less the research required to determine where these plants might be, or the missions training to identify the kind of churches that might be required or the people groups who might be reached, simply did not exist. There seemed to exist a combination of revival expectancy and a kind of myopia that tended to suggest that the very declaration of the goal with a sufficient faith content would somehow cause it to be accomplished.

This is not to say that some real attempts to plant significant numbers of churches were not made. New Frontiers had already committed their network to an extensive church planting operation and are on record as indicating that the Challenge 2000 initiative helped to give a legitimacy to their activity. The Methodist Church committed itself to planting one new church for every district – a goal of 600 new church plants. The Salvation Army also initiated processes to focus on church planting. In fact every major denomination had official plans, policies or reports endorsing church planting within a couple of years of that first Congress.

Even though the goal was not reached, an attempt was made to plant churches which otherwise might not have been made. Most denominations made some attempt to church plant following the 1992 Congress. The URC, for example, adopted the DAWN principles and began to church plant which it might otherwise not have done. In general, the DAWN processes convinced many churches of the diversity of models of church planting as compared with the 'clergyman and a green field model' which had tended to apply to that date.

In 1995 a second (and final) Congress was held in Nottingham and some 1,000 leaders attended again from right across the churches. However, here a major opportunity was lost. The process in the Congress included breaking into reasonably small regional groups, each of which was provided with their share of the 20,000 goal, divided on a population basis. This clearly highlighted the ridiculous nature of the goals in almost every region. However, there was a combination of inadequate feedback of these findings together with unwillingness among the Challenge 2000 leaders to grasp the nettle and admit that they had got it wrong and must revert to some realism. One result was a massive demoralization and loss of confidence in the process at the grass roots where the mission energy needed to be.

As early as 1996, there were signs that many of the attempts at church planting seemed to run out of energy and simply stopped. This was not uniformly true across all the denominations and streams but in terms of what might have been seen as the beginnings of a broad movement, the momentum was lost.

An examination of the experience of one of the groups that took the goals most seriously helps to understand why the energy ran out. The Assemblies of God committed to planting 1,000 new congregations by the year 2000. That represented more than a doubling of the number of congregations that they already had. A good beginning was made and by the end of three years some 200 new congregations had been started. By any standards, given that it had taken nearly 70 years to begin the first 600 congregations this was an astonishing achievement. At this point they were clearly on target to achieve their goal of 600 church plants. But then the planting stopped. Worse still, some of the new outreach/planting attempts closed and most of the other new congregations did not continue to grow and indeed showed signs of the very kind of problems that many of the older congregations had and which church planting was intended to overcome.

The actual number of churches that emerged from the 200 was in fact 63. Later 13 of these closed leaving 50 new churches. However, in that time a further 30 historical churches closed leaving a net gain of 20. What had gone wrong? One way of explaining the process is to suggest that these first 200 plants represented the only 'easy hits' that were available. In other words, many of these congregations consisted of collecting disaffected Christians from other churches and collecting them into new Assemblies of God. Those disaffected Christians tended to bring their disaffections with them and so what resulted was a series of new congregations that were fundamentally unhealthy. This may be an exaggeration and indeed there were undoubtedly some good, strong, mission-based church plants with good records in terms of winning new Christians. But where these existed they were the minority.

In other words, attention had been given to the 'how' part of church planting but very little to the 'what' issues. Much the same kind of experience applied to other denominations and networks too, so that by the late 1990s the goal of planting 20,000 new churches had slipped quietly away.

Challenge 2000 as an organization was moribund and it looked as if yet another initiative in the Decade of Evangelism had simply failed.

Fortunately that was not the end of the story. The immediate consequence of the ebbing of church planting energy was the quiet development of a process of genuine missionary reflection. At last, the 'what' issues were being faced. The church in the UK has been through a period of time when it has asked some profound questions about the nature of the church. The nature of what the church is and should be has surfaced in a whole variety of manifestations, many of them highly experimental and provisional as structures. Many of these are being recorded as part of an Anglican initiative called 'Fresh Expressions'. There are reasons for thinking that similar questions were being addressed in other parts of the West during the same period of time manifested particularly in what has become known as the Emerging Church but witnessed also in the issues addressed by the Gospel and Our Culture movement.

The provisional experiments represented by initiatives such as Fresh Expressions are encouraging but they still leave open the question, is it wise or even desirable to think of planting significant numbers of churches in a situation like the UK where there are already large numbers of churches present? In particular, does the existence of a highly developed parish situation, such as in the case of the Church of England, which is not likely to go away in the foreseeable future, really mean we should be placing all of our emphasis on issues of renewal and revitalization and not on church planting? There is at least one study that suggests that the decline of the Church of England can be traced back to the overprovision of buildings in the late nineteenth century. Although I don't think we need to take that particular study too seriously, is there nevertheless a theoretical capacity point which applies in Western contexts?

The case for planting

I want to suggest that there are at least five good reasons for taking church planting seriously. First, there is the obvious point that populations are not static. Not only is the building of new housing stock in new locations a prominent feature of the Western world, it is also the case that high levels of immigration all across the Western world provide at least the opportunity and need for church planting.

Second, church planting helps with the normal cycle of renewal. Not all churches live for ever. Some seem to have natural life cycles after which they come to a close. The reasons for their closure may be diverse but the reality is that thousands of churches all across the Western world do close, only to be replaced by other churches, sometimes even using the same building but serving a different people group, or even serving the same people group but in a different style.

Third, church planting is a natural part of the redefinition of the overall make-up of the church. Whether we notice it or not, the reality of church life is that the 'centre' or 'mainstream' is constantly being redefined. We usually do not notice it because it takes place over a generation or two. For example, in the United States of America at the beginning of the nineteenth century the dominant church groups were the Presbyterians, the Episcopalians and the Congregationalists. The Methodists and the Baptists were insignificant sects. By the end of the nineteenth century the Methodists and the Baptists had outgrown the former mainstream denominations and thus helped to reshape the centre or mainstream of Christianity.

Lest we are tempted to think that this kind of shift is only possible in a situation like North America where the frontier was constantly expanding, a more recent illustration from the United Kingdom serves to make the point. In 1972 the United Reformed Church came into being as a union between the Congregationalist and the English Presbyterians. The membership was cited at that time as 192,136. In the same year the Assemblies of God numbered 28,000 – just 10 per cent of the total. The United Reformed Church was regarded as a major mainstream denomination and the Assemblies of God as a peripheral group. In 2004 the comparative memberships were 81,638 for the United Reformed Church and 68,000 for the Assemblies of God[7]. It is likely that in the next decade the Assemblies of God will be larger than the United Reformed Church. Even more spectacularly, it is possible that in the next twenty years, a group of churches that was not even in being in 1972, New Frontiers, will be significantly larger than the United Reformed Church. These growing groups are church planting their way into the mainstream.

Fourth, church planting offers an area of missional experiment. Because we are living between paradigms, it is foolish to pretend that we already have well defined ideas about what the church of the coming century will look like. That is not a good reason for doing nothing until we have clear ideas and well formed future models. It is a reason for treating our activity as provisional and experimental. Church planting offers an arena in which that experimentation can find room for expression.

Fifth, many of the disciplines contained within church planting can be applied to existing churches as part of a revitalization process. Where the elements of church planting expertise are applied consciously and systematically to an existing congregation, we might be able to describe the rebirth of a congregation as a replanting exercise. The need to replant is probably just as urgent and necessary as the need to plant many completely new congregations.

Notes
1. This issue is debated in more detail in, Robinson, Martin, *The Faith of the Unbeliever*, Monarch, 1994
2. The five marks of mission were agreed at the Lambeth Conference attended by the world-wide communion of Anglican bishops in 1988. They are:
    i. To proclaim the Good News of the Kingdom
    ii. To teach, baptise and nurture new believers
    iii. To respond to human need by loving service
    iv. To seek to transform unjust structures of society
    v. To strive to safeguard the integrity of creation and sustain and renew the life of the earth
3. The debate about the marginalisation of the church in the public square is well summarised in, Newbigin, Lesslie, *The Gospel in a Pluralist Society*, SPCK, 1989.
4. Scruton, Roger, *The West and the Rest: Gobalization and the Terrorist Threat*, ISI Books, 2002, p. viii.
5. Jack, Ian, *The Conflict Between Religion and Free Speech*, Guardian, 1/1/05, p. 7.
6. Appleyard, Bryan, *Beyond Belief*, Sunday Times Review Section, 27/3/05, p. 1.
7. The figures for the United Reformed Church come from their published year books. The figures for the Assemblies of God are more problematic in that they don't keep official figures but they have been estimated by the Christian Research Association and kindly provided to the author by Heather Wraight.

Chapter Two
The Changing Shape of Church

A conference with the name Mission 21, to be held 7–10 March 2006 in Sheffield, England, is intended to be a major event on the theme of church planting. It is hoped that many hundreds of church planters will attend. As the planning process began, a serious question arose that went straight to the heart of the intent of the event. Is it possible to use the term 'church planting'? Clearly Christians in most parts of the world do use the term very intentionally and freely. What then lay behind such a concern?

Those who asked the question felt that the phrase 'church planting' was so associated with a model of church planting that had been found wanting in the 1990s in the UK, that it would be better to find another term. Various alternatives were on offer: simple church, fresh expressions of church, emerging church and mission-shaped church, to name a few. As you might imagine it was not easy to find agreement because each of the alternatives carried with them a significant other agenda which connected with church planting but also contained a variety of other suppositions and contentions.

This debate reveals the need to rehabilitate the term 'church planting'. The heart of the problem had been the association of church planting with somewhat mechanistic methodologies relating to planting and with models of church which simply replicated the largely failed structures and models of the past. More of that which had already failed was not going to produce different results. But something slightly different does seem to be entering the picture. A number of observers of the church scene, particularly those associated with what are often known as the home mission departments of denominations, have noticed a significant upsurge of church planting in recent years. This recent upsurge seems to have some different emphases than in the past.

This growth in church planting activity can be broadly categorized in three ways. First, that which is known within the existing denominations and networks.[1] There is no uniform pattern across the denominations, but we can make a distinction between those groupings which have made a conscious and clear strategic decision to church plant in order to grow, and those who are seeing church planting take place more as local and personal initiatives. For example, in Great Britain, groups as diverse as the Salvation Army, New Frontiers, Vineyard and the Fellowship of Independent Evangelical Churches all have well developed strategies and investment in church planting. Should they be successful in their activities, then over time they will become part of the process of establishing a new mainstream in church life.

By contrast, some major denominations, the Anglicans, the Methodists and the Baptists could be described as 'planting friendly' but without a single national strategy. Much activity takes place and it is certainly encouraged but it does not form part of a unified plan of action. Often the initiatives that are encouraged consist of attempts at cross-cultural church planting, usually in difficult inner-city settings. The Baptist initiative Urban Expression represents a good example of this kind of planting.

In the United States, some of the conscious church planting activity of a few denominations is making a major difference to the profile of those same denominations. Two examples from groupings which are historically related makes the point. First, the Disciples of Christ (sometimes called the Christian Church and based in Indianapolis). The Disciples are one of the mainstream historic churches in the United States that has been in long-term, serious decline. Numbers have dropped in the United States and Canada from well over a million in 1968 to 882,721 by 1998. In recent years they have adopted a programme of church planting designed to add 2,000 congregations by the year 2020. To date they are ahead of their target and look certain to become the first of the historic, mainstream churches to reverse long-term decline.

The Christian Churches / Churches of Christ (Independent) grouping, using a church planting agency called Stadia, has an even more ambitious goal. While this rather more evangelical group had never been in decline, it has certainly teetered near the edge for a few decades. Indeed, without the remarkable development of a large number of megachurches in their midst, decline would almost certainly have begun in the closing decades of the twentieth century. However, in recent years they have set a goal of planting 5,500 churches by the year 2025 and they too seem to be exceeding the growth plan that they have established. One consequence of this activity has been to place the Christian Churches (Independent) as the fastest growing religious group in the United States of America after the Mormons. That is a remarkable turnaround for a group of churches that had almost become moribund.

The second broad category relates to that which lies on the edge of what churches are normally engaged in. The Anglican researcher George Lings, who is employed by the Church Army, collects stories and data that illustrate many of these experimental engagements in mission and church planting.[2] His website www.encountersontheedge.org.uk points to stories of church planting that don't fit the norm. The actual stories are contained in a regular newsletter. The categories offered by George often relate more to the location of church, for example midweek church, café-style church or school congregations, as well as the particular people groups who might be reached by a more flexible approach to church. In many ways these are extensions of what the church might be expected to do. George Lings includes in his definition of a church plant the possibility of new alternative worship congregations. There could be some debate as to whether such expressions, fresh, creative or merely imitated can credibly be described as church planting but they certainly do reflect the kind of creative, experimental and provisional attempts to be church that one might expect to emerge in the locus between paradigms.

There are many of these more 'edgy' expressions of church emerging from the work of parachurch agencies who in the past have concentrated more on evangelism than on mission and church planting. What's the difference? Evangelistic agencies, whether aimed at youth or at other sections of the population have traditionally seen themselves as winning people to Christ and then feeding them into existing churches. The idea that such an agency might set up a church plant that is unconnected to an existing church strikes at the very heart of the contract between parachurch agencies and their supporters. For this reason, these experiments are not much heralded yet they are increasingly taking place.

The third broad category is what we might call beyond the edge.[3] These are expressions of church that are arising spontaneously, without the involvement of existing denominations or structures. Some have written of these kinds of people movements in terms of Church Planting Movements. The terminology is not exactly startling but what it refers to is the spontaneous spread of the Christian faith among people groups such that churches arise from the many converts. That is slightly different from the idea that one plants culturally relevant churches in order to win people to faith. Are those kinds of movements happening in the Western world? Arguably they are taking place among the many immigrant peoples in the Western world. The previously mentioned Disciples of Christ denomination is seeing its greatest church planting success among Hispanics near the border with Mexico. The mushrooming of ethnic church plants in some of the boroughs of London are almost hidden to the casual observer yet when researched reveal astonishing levels of conversion growth and congregational multiplication.

It is hard to know what you don't know but investigative research is beginning to reveal the development of what some are calling 'simple church', or sometimes 'home churches'. At its very basic level simple church consists of home groups dedicated to developing relationships with those who are not Christians, engaging in evangelism and then in discipleship processes without the aid of structures beyond that of homes. In this model, new converts quickly become the most effective evangelists. Two of the best exponents of this approach are Felicity and Tony Dale.[4]

The advocates of simple church suggest that as many as 1 million Christians are meeting in home churches in the United States. That figure makes no distinction between those who are meeting together because they are disillusioned with the established church and who have no missional impact and those who are very intentional in evangelism and the multiplication of disciples. One website based in the UK makes the claim:

> Something is happening across Britain today: a new kind of church is beginning to appear; increasing numbers of Christians are starting to gather in homes, colleges and work places. Living out a 24-7 faith, they are missionally focused with a 'go to them' dynamic instead of a 'come to us' invita-

tion. These churches are small, fluid, organic, reproducible and most of all simple; so simple that any believer would respond by saying 'I could do that!'[5]

How many Christians are involved in these kinds of groups? One researcher, Alexander Campbell, has engaged in some detailed analysis of a number of specific towns, cities and rural areas in Britain and has concluded that there are probably around ten organic communities (gathering as a church) for every 100,000 people in the population. His view is that the average size of these groups is around twelve people. That extrapolates to a total figure of 6,000 groups with 72,000 people. It is too early to say if these figures are accurate but they are the best that are available to date.[6]

Clearly there are other questions that need to be asked. In particular, are these groups growing in terms of conversion growth or do they mostly consist of those who have deserted Evangelical, Pentecostal or Charismatic churches – the EPCs described in the book *Churchless Faith*. Further questions need to be asked and some additional research is being conducted by Alexander Campbell.

Clearly there is overlap between these various categories and it soon becomes clear that some of the same leaders, thinkers, organizations and publications are cited by those from all three of these streams or approaches. In particular, the work of DAWN, of Cell church and the organizations that connect with these manifestations of church planting are nearly always present on the various websites. That reality leads to the question, are these various manifestations of life actually just different forms of a single movement or is there a case that these are competitive and ultimately irreconcilable attempts to manifest the future church?

Some obvious themes emerge from all of these various manifestations of church planting. Five themes are worth mentioning at this stage. First, there is an undoubted common frustration with what has become known as an 'attractional' model of church. The term 'programme' church seeks to convey the same core idea. The root of the objection is not the idea that a church should be somehow unattractive or indeed abandon programmes that meet the needs of the local community. It is rather the idea that the life of such a church is operated by a staff of professionals who effectively 'entertain' a largely passive congregation.

There is a widespread conviction, supported by some research, that such congregations are usually ineffective at reaching non-Christians and all too effective at attracting Christians from other churches. The 'attractional' tag hits at the ingathering of those who do not desire to be mobilized and is seen as the very antithesis of movement. There is not an objection to any church which is able to attract large numbers of non-Christians. Curiously there are some churches which from many perspectives look exactly like the programmatic attractional church, attacked so vociferously by those with a missional heart, and yet which do manage to attract significant numbers of non-Christians who then are mobilized in mission. Such churches are rare indeed but where they do exist they are often involved as sending churches – sending missionaries overseas and church planters to surrounding areas.

Second, there is a desire for an authentic spirituality. Many of those who appear to be retaining faith but dropping out of regular church worship, seem to be exhibiting weariness with forms of worship that seem not to connect with the soul. It would be easy at this point to be cynical and accuse such church dropouts as exhibiting the classic symptoms of consumer boredom – searching in this case for the next spiritual high. But that would be a facile account of the genuine search of these individuals for a God encounter that leads to an authentic spirituality that engages with the world.

Third, the desire for authentic spirituality finds further expression in a longing for a spirituality that contains cultural relevance. These are not believers who are looking for other worldly pietism so much as forms of faith that affirm the good in the culture that their friends, family and colleagues inhabit. They have a deep desire to see their neighbours connect with the Christian community and see only too clearly the chasm that exists between the life of the church and the lives of those they seek to reach with the good news of the gospel.

Fourth, discipleship is always high on the agenda. That is not to say that discipleship is always well done. Indeed, one could argue that discipleship is the one area of struggle for the whole church around the world. The teaching of the habits of the heart that mould character has become a lost art for many Christian communities. The desire to engage in discipleship well rather than its actual accomplishment might be a more realistic descriptor.

Fifth, the hoped for outcome of good discipleship processes is the effective mobilization of significant numbers of believers. The development of mobilized believers, operating as mature disciples, leads to the generation of movement. The growth of movement leads to the kind of culturally relevant evangelism that has the potential, not just to change individual lives but to transform, in time, a society, a culture. What we have described is a kind of provisional DNA which can interact with many models, cultures, styles and formats to produce significantly different approaches to church planting while retaining a beating missional heart.

The thrust of the above argument suggests that the adoption of a missional DNA can potentially take place in all three of the categories or streams outlined earlier. The diversity of models and approaches represents both a strength and an honest admission that we cannot yet know if a particular approach is going to be more effective than others. This is the time to be both agnostic about whether a particular model is better than any other and generous in terms of recognizing that opting for a 'mixed economy' in terms of forms and styles, while undoubtedly pragmatic, is also the best we can do at this stage in the re-imagining of the shape of the church.[7]

In the confusion of approaches something of significance does seem to be emerging. That is not to say that everything with the label 'emerging' represents the future. Indeed, while remaining pragmatic and generous it is also the time to be discerning. We do not have to be agnostic about everything. Some judgments can and must be made. The term 'emerging' covers a very wide range of church life. Some commentators from within the emerging scene have noted that there can be a confusion of style over and against substance. There seems to be some feeling that not all that has emerged from the alternative worship scene is healthy. Indeed one could argue that to place too much emphasis on worship style over and against an interaction with the broader community can lead to the kind of 'boutique' church that is not much more than 'this is how me and my friends like to do church'. Too little regard to the accessibility of the worshipping community on the part of those who are not Christian can hardly be described as missional.

Undoubtedly there are many from within the 'emerging' church that exhibit a missional heart. Is it perhaps time to make common cause with other streams that might at first sight look different in terms of form and style but which actually contain the same missional DNA? Those who have encountered ethnic churches in the West know only too well that the forms displayed by such churches can look very traditional but missional life is undoubtedly (though not inevitably) present. Might this be the time to stress similarities of heart rather than emphasize differences in style?

Our ability to make such common cause concerning the future (or we might say agreement about the solutions to our problems) will be somewhat influenced by our analysis of the problem itself. How do we understand our present situation? There does seem to be a fairly fundamental disagreement about whether we are engaged in renewal or revolution. Let me explain what I mean and why this makes a difference to our church planting strategies.

There is a view, sometimes associated with the emerging church, that the fundamental problem for the church flows from the phenomenon of Christendom. Briefly stated, this view suggests that the church was a dynamic movement up until the time of Constantine and then made a fateful compact with the power of the state. The effect of that agreement was on the one hand to increase the influence and numerical success of the church but on the other to compromise something of the heart of the Christian faith such that the church tended to misuse power. The accommodation with privilege caused the church to adopt a structure that reflected power. The actions of the church moved towards coercion and a pattern of activity that has brought shame to the followers of Christ. Although coercion in the matter of conversion was by no means the norm, the fact that it did take place reflected the fact that it could take place largely because of the patronage of the state. The concern of those who look at these developments with dismay are reflected in the following questions taken from the book *Post-Christendom*: '... Had Christianity conquered the Empire or had the Empire co-opted and domesticated Christianity? What price did the church pay for imperial patronage? The gains were obvious but what were the losses?'[8]

The broad case against the development of Christendom suggests that something of immense and intrinsic value was lost by the Christian community and that the resulting gains were not worth the loss. Mission became a form of colonialism. The spread of the Empire was seen as identical to the spread of a broad Christian civilization. In short, the mission of the church was fatally compromised and only now, with the ending of Christendom, does the church have a chance of recovering its true identity and message. For those who take this view, Christendom has been around ever since the time of Constantine and is only now coming to a dramatic end.

The view that a change of immense significance has taken place is reinforced by the writings of those such as Callum Brown who take the view that the recent decline of Christianity in the West is both unprecedented and completely new. For Brown, the significance of developments since the 1960s is that Christianity has, for the first time in history, failed to engage in the normal cycle of renewal that connects one generation with another in the faith: 'The cycle of inter-generational renewal of Christian affiliation, a cycle which had for so many centuries tied the people however closely or loosely to the churches and to Christian moral benchmarks, was permanently disrupted in the "swinging sixties"'.[9]

If you accept this radical view of Christian history then the failure of Christendom is not a tragedy but an opportunity. The ending of Christendom signals the recovery of an earlier and more pristine form of Christianity. It is not possible to build on these failed foundations; the time has come to begin again, to recover a new missional imagination that will create a completely new form of the church. Some who take this view claim that this new form of non-institutional church is even now emerging all round the world. The research of Barrett is cited as offering numerical support to this view of reality.[10] What is called for is revolution – the scrapping of a failed and flawed past and an entirely new start.

Those who are familiar with accounts of church history will recognize the preceding account as a largely Anabaptist view of history. There are well documented responses to the Anabaptist argument. This isn't the place to review them thoroughly, but they can be found in the work of those such as Oliver O'Donovan who points out that while there may be some problems with the excesses of Christendom, it also produced much that was thoroughly good.[11] Moreover, they challenge Anabaptists by insisting that the Anabaptist position only functions as a reaction or a riposte, in itself it does not take the issue of power and the Christian response to it sufficiently seriously.

For the purposes of this debate there are some other more worrying problems with the argument. Three points need to be made. First, the idea that Christendom has been a single and consistent state of affairs from Constantine until today simply does not fit the facts. Even if the church has had a long-term affair with Christendom, one is bound to ask, which version you are talking about, because there have been several. Constantine was not the first ruler to arrive at an understanding between church and State. That first happened in Armenia. The Eastern story has been different from the Western story. The early form of Western Christendom had more to do with Pope Gregory than with Constantine. The later and more developed form of late medieval Christendom where the church enjoyed a degree of actual temporal power has been very different from the expressions of Christendom in modernity. In recent times, utilitarian privilege rather than actual power has tended to be the key defining feature of the relationship between the diverse Christian community and the state.

Second, the idea that there was once a pure form of Christianity that existed before Constantine that we can somehow now recover, is commonly known as restorationism. This notion has come in many forms in the last several hundred years and it has always ended in disappointment. The idea that the history of Christianity is of little worth and that we can simply reach back to the pages of the New Testament or to the experience of the early church without regard to the centuries that have shaped us does not stand up to the critical and sometimes bitter analysis of experience. That, of course, does not stop new generations from making the attempt but neither does it invalidate the lesson.

Third, there is another way of viewing the historical picture. David Bosch, borrowing from Hans Kung, talks of the history of mission and the Christian church in terms of a series of major paradigm shifts. For Bosch there have been at least six of these shifts. He describes them as

1. The apocalyptic paradigm of primitive Christianity.
2. The Hellenistic paradigm of the patristic period.
3. The medieval Roman Catholic paradigm.
4. The Protestant (Reformation) paradigm.
5. The modern Enlightenment paradigm.
6. The emerging ecumenical paradigm.[12]

It does not really matter whether Bosch or Kung has rightly identified the various paradigms in church history. My suspicion is that the emerging ecumenical paradigm is ill-named and will turn out very differently than Bosch imagined. It is also a very Eurocentric view of history and probably does not take sufficient account of the Celtic contribution even within the West. However, the key concept that the church has had to missionally reinvent itself in response to massive shifts in culture is a helpful notion. The idea is not so much renewal which refers to processes that take place within these larger paradigms, nor revolution which imagines a radical break between one epoch and another. The concept of missional reimagination allows for continuity and for dynamic change.

Those who take the more radical view of the place of Christendom object that Bosch is operating entirely within the orbit of Christendom and is blinded to its effects. The problem with that stance is that it fails to answer the key question as to what precisely it is that Christendom contains that needs to be confronted and overcome. Moreover, such a radical view fails to take account of the fact that Christendom looked very different in modernity than it did in the medieval world. It may have been called Christendom in both eras but does this refer to any more than the idea that Christianity operated as the primary inspiration for the social imagination of the age? That locus as the provider of moral and cultural direction gave Christianity a position of influence rather than power. Who can argue that the Mennonite Church, scourge of Constantine, has not actually been part of Christendom itself viewed in this much more limited and utilitarian way. It is this version of Christendom that Philip Jenkins is alluding to in his book *The Next Christendom*.

This can lead one to wonder about the usefulness of the shorthand term Christendom. It is likely that we have come to use the term, not so much as a comment on the period from Constantine till today but more as a mindset, a way of looking at the institution, the church, which prevents the church from acting in a missional way. What we may be talking about is not a single way of being church for the last 1,700 years – those who know the diversity of the church over that period would see that as unlikely. Rather, there is an attitude that prevails in the declining years of any institution which acts against innovation, imagination, creativity and development. The fixation with preservation as compared with the servicing of a vision can even cause an institution to hold the foolish perspective, 'we must find a vision in order to flourish'. That is entirely the wrong conclusion. A better orientation would be, how can we change in order to understand and serve the vision that brought us into being in the first place?

What I am suggesting is that the church enters phases when it seeks to engage imaginatively in the kind of mission that will change the world in which it is set. Usually, though not always, the church succeeds in making this kind of adaptation and then becomes a victim of its own success. In short, its very success brings influence and that influence can bring dominance and even arrogance. As it enters such a time, its connection with the existing culture needs to be renewed. Mostly, the church is able to renew its life but occasionally there come challenges which are deeper than mere renewal. The culture itself shifts to such an extent that no easy reconnection is possible. At such times there needs to come a new, far reaching and highly imaginative way of rethinking everything about the church. As chapter one argues, we are in such a time.

Does this debate really matter? Is there really such a difference between seeing the past merely as Christendom that needs to be overthrown or to see the past as a series of paradigm shifts that bring challenges to our creative imagination? I suspect that it does matter in a number of regards. First, to fixate on the wrong enemy is potentially to miss the challenge of our times. We cannot afford to waste that amount of energy. Second, the dichotomy between revolution or renewal is a false one that stops us placing our investment where it needs to be in the generation of new movements. Genuine movements connect with the past but reinterpret the past to such an extent that the essential genius of the gospel is recast in new clothes for the new culture. The term emerging church is a wonderful term if it describes that which is emerging to connect with an equally emergent new culture. If it is simply about the aesthetics of worship or defined by what it is against it will miss the tide.

That then is why church planting movements are so important. Church planting conceived as an instrument to renew that which has been will fail. Church planting that becomes a vehicle for the creation of movements can serve us well.

Notes

1. Number of churches started in the U.K. as an annual decadal average"

1980's	290
Early 1990's	230
Late 1990's	110

    This reflects the accuracy of the perception of a grass roots movement in the 1980's moving forward into the early part of the 1990's.

It also reveals the extent of the church planting crisis in the late 1990's. This information comes from the Christian Research Association and I am grateful to Peter Brierley for supplying it. More detailed information which gives a denominational breakdown is available from the *UK Christian Handbook: Religious Trends 5*, Christian Research Association, 2005.

2. Information on experimental church life is collected partly by George Lings and partly by Fresh Expressions. George and the Fresh Expressions team are in active co-operation. The Fresh Expression web site gives an indication of the breadth of activity.
3. A research project on experiments beyond the edge has been commissioned by the Mission 21 church planting event. Preliminary findings have been presented to the organising committee and a full report will be available after the event. It may be published if sufficient interest is aroused, at the very least an indication of results will be available on the Together in Mission website, www.togetherinmission.org
4. For more on Simple Church see Chapter 9 in this book beginning page 157.
5. See, www.simplechurch.co.uk, however the site is always changing and the particular phrase that I extracted may not still be posted.
6. See note 3 above.
7. The term "mixed economy" has been widely used by the Archbishop of Canterbury to indicate that it is possible to see experimental church forms running side by side with more traditional forms. Many in the Anglican church have taken this to mean that parish boundaries will be loosened such that it will not be possible for clergy to prevent neighbouring parishes from engaging in church planting initiatives in "their patch".
8. Murray-Williams, Stuart, *Post-Christendom: Church and Mission in a Strange New World*, Paternoster, 2004, p. 44.
9. Brown, Callum, *The Death of Christian Britain*, Routledge, 2001, p 1.
10. Alan Hirsch has a new book in preparation which will be published by Baker in 2006. He has kindly shown me the manuscript and he uses figures that Barratt suggests for numbers of Christians operating outside of denominational structures, in this kind of way and he is not alone in doing so.
11. O'Donovan, Oliver, *The Desire of the Nations: Rediscovering the Roots of Political Theology*, 1996.
12. Bosch David, *Transforming Mission*, Orbis, 1991, p. 181.
13. Jenkins, Philip, *The Next Christendom*, OUP, 2002.

Chapter Three
The Art of Church Planting

We have spent some time looking at the broad sweep of church planting, of its current progress in the West, the problems associated with it, the issues it raises and the intrinsic relationship between church planting, mission and movement. It is necessary now to begin to look at some of the issues that surround what is planted, where it might be planted and who is doing the planting.

In my first book on church planting, written in conjunction with Stuart Christine, we looked at the issues of what to plant and where to plant in two completely different chapters.[1] Looking back on those chapters I tend to think now that they were overly mechanistic. In truth there is a complex relationship between who is planting, the model that is being adopted, the sending agent and the community that is finally selected. Although in theory some church planting agencies have an approach which looks rather rigid and uniform on paper, in reality the process is much more complex and organic.

Over the last fifteen years I have talked with dozens of church planters and have nearly always asked them about their personal journey. I am particularly interested in how they came to plant precisely where they planted. As you might imagine, no two stories have ever been exactly the same. Nevertheless, some common themes do emerge:

1. My denomination, network or local church were recruiting planters. I responded, was accepted and then I was sent.
2. I never planned to plant a church, it just seemed to happen around me.
3. I had long felt a call to plant a church and so I found a good place to begin and got started.
4. We saw a great opportunity to plant a church in a nearby area and it seemed right to take it.
5. I had a growing concern for a particular area and came to believe that a church plant would help to make a difference there.
6. I have been a church planter all my life. Once I plant one church I look for an opportunity to plant another.
7. I was contacted by a group who wanted to plant a church and invited me to lead them.
8. I was the minister of a church that was involved in church planting and eventually felt it right to lead one of the plants myself.
9. I had a concern for a particular people group and felt that a church plant among them would be of value.
10. Large numbers of people had come to Christ through some of our ministries. They didn't easily fit in the church that I was part of and so we felt it would be good to begin a church for them.

The list could continue for many pages but even though these short statements sum up the key characteristic of the church planting call, they do not describe the story. In most cases there is a process that lies behind these summary statements. An initial impression or invitation is followed by a period of questioning. Confirmation is sought, in prayer and sometimes through prophecies, the encouragement of others or through particular practical circumstances such as the raising of funds. The process of questioning and confirmation can take place over long or short periods of time. The details of every journey are unique. Whatever the particular story there are usually four polarities which can be described in the following quadrant:

Recruited and sent	Intentional search
Opportunity arises	Locally available

You can plot where on the quadrant you feel your journey best fits. As you plot that journey you can think through the strengths and weaknesses of your situation in relation to the issues listed below.

1. **Recruited and sent.** The strength of this polarity is that an organization or a network is working with the planter. Hopefully there will be a support mechanism in relation to mentoring and coaching. It is possible that some kind of selection process will have been used to assess suitability for church planting and for cultural 'fit' in relation to the situation for which the planter has been recruited or to which they are being sent. Question to ask: how good a support structure does the organization actually have – do they have sufficient experience to be responsible overseers, or will other help be needed?
2. **Locally available.** The planter will be well known by those they are going to work with. Likewise the planter will know what they are going to. In that sense there are no surprises. Question to ask: what training will be needed, including exposure to other situations in order to prepare adequately for the task?

The Art of Church Planting 51

3. **Intentional search.** There is an opportunity to engage in high quality demographic research to give the plant a strong possibility of success. Question to ask: how does the planter know that this is the situation that God is leading them to?
4. **Opportunity arises.** There can be a strong sense that God is at work, opening doors and giving opportunity. Question to ask: is this opportunity a need which is being responded to or really a call from God? Remember, every need is not a call.

Choosing a place to plant

Plotting where you fit on the above quadrant will help you to gain a grasp of the issues that surround where you might plant. But there are also a number of other issues relating to the precise nature of your call that will greatly influence your choice of a planting location. In short, the nature of your journey strongly influences the choice of planting location. The following stories do not represent an exhaustive list of case histories in relation to the planting possibilities but they do give a strong indicator of the issues you might face. The following illustrations are all composites of many actual situations and so they reflect real planting situations even if they are not accurate as single stories. As stories they all reflect the acknowledged models listed below.

Sent as a couple to another area

Julie and Arthur were effective local leaders in a lively and growing church. Their denomination was committed to church planting, and knowing that this was the case, their local church approached them to ask if they had considered becoming church planters. They were willing and, after some prayer and discussion with the denomination, a particular city was located. Why was this city chosen? From the denomination's perspective, it fitted the population profile that they had adopted as part of their strategic analysis, there was no other church of their denomination in that city and yet there was another sister church in a nearby city who might provide some help.

From the perspective of the planters, they did not feel a strong call to that particular city but having prayed and visited the city a few times they felt a peace about it working. They needed to find secular employment in the new location while they established their strategy and began to generate their foundations for the new plant. They were able to find jobs easily. That circumstantial provision acted to reinforce their sense of peace. Work has now begun on relationship evangelism with a view to generating some small groups meeting in homes and in identifying some existing Christians who might wish to assist in the new work.

Sent as a team

A church planting organization had identified a needy, urban area where there was no effective Christian presence. Some work on social care projects had identified an openness to the gospel provided that it was culturally relevant. Three couples were recruited as church planters to lead a new church. At the point of recruitment, the location for the church plant had already been selected and so the team members had the opportunity to explore the neighbourhood and see if they felt a sense of call to that particular location and project. They were to earn their living by working on social care projects in and near the estate where the work was to be planted.

One of the couples, Stan and Claire, were appointed as the team leaders and they met for a time as a team of six people. Over a few months a number of others (around fifteen) who were already Christians opted to join them in the project. The larger team met regularly as a whole group but also in three home groups. Once they had established enough good relationships in the target area, they launched a regular public worship service meeting in a local school. They now have around sixty people meeting. All who have joined since the public launch are new Christians.

Called to a particular people group

Raj and Rachel live in a predominately Asian neighbourhood in a large British city. Their jobs are such that they could live anywhere in that city and they made a conscious choice to live in an Asian area. Raj became a Christian some years ago prior to his marriage and has maintained many strong friendships and family connections within the Asian community. Both Raj and Rachel have a concern for young professional Asians who are wondering what it means to be an Asian born in Britain. Many are interested in spiritual issues and are nominally members of their own traditional faith group. Some are Muslim, others are Sikh and some Hindu by background.

Flowing from these many strong friendships and good conversations about spiritual matters, a small but growing home group began. Later it grew too large for a home and moved into a nearby community hall. The format is simple: food, friendship, some very informal and contemporary worship which seeks to mix Asian styles of music, dance and meditation and some reflection on Bible stories. Some individuals are becoming Christians but it is all very low-key. Rachel and Raj support themselves through other work. Some local churches help to meet the expenses of the group and leaders from some of these churches provide an oversight group.

The independent (catalytic) planter

Derek Shepherd has planted churches all of his life. On average he has planted one church every five years. He is well known in his denomination as a planter, and over the years a number of churches and individuals have supported his ministry financially. How does Derek choose a new place to plant a church? Even Derek finds that a hard question to answer! Looking back there are some similarities in the places that he has chosen. He seems always to look for areas of new housing. They have always been private housing with middle-class people who are not wealthy but are aspiring to improve their lifestyle. These new estates do not contain just a few hundred people, more likely 10,000 or thereabouts. He does no research but has usually relied on the 'intelligence' that has come from friends he knows in the denomination.

These friends are important in a number of ways. Not only do they point out a potentially good new area that needs a church plant, they also invite him to come to that area and pledge that if he comes they will be founder members of the church plant. Usually there are no more than a dozen people in the inviting group, so how does Derek obtain the numbers needed to launch a new church plant?

Derek is a great believer in using huge amounts of shoe leather. He goes to those places in the community where he can meet people. Sometimes he joins clubs, neighbourhood watch schemes, or becomes a local school governor. He has the knack of talking to everyone and becoming well known. He is always willing to lend a hand, make a contact for someone, offer advice and just be a listening ear. On occasion he goes door to door, introducing himself and offering to pray for people. His personality is such that he is often well received. He has a winning smile and a pleasant manner. People can't help liking Derek. Out of these multiple contacts emerge the individuals who become the core group for his embryonic church plant. Almost always the new church uses a community hall or school.

Derek only stays for three to five years. In the first year following the plant he identifies his successor as minister and invites them to work with him as his assistant with a view to them remaining after he has gone. Because he raises his own support, the congregation are able to support Derek's assistant. Most of the churches that Derek has planted are still in being and the majority now have their own building, partly paid for by the local membership and partly by the denomination.

Working with ethnic revival

Grace was a lawyer and a lay leader in her local church. She is a Nigerian and at that time was working in London. For some time Grace had a strong sense that she would be moving to another city. Eventually there came an opportunity to take a new post in another English city. The leaders in her London church prayed for her and with her. Some with a prophetic gift felt that God was calling her to a new job but also to plant a church. When she arrived in her new city and home she began to contact fellow Nigerians and discovered that many were looking for a spiritual home and were looking to her for leadership.

After much prayer and fasting and with much encouragement from seeing answers to her prayers – people being healed, delivered and converted, she agreed that God was leading her to begin a new church. She sought advice and recognition from the leaders of the denomination that she had previously been a member of when in London. They gave her encouragement and the new work was launched. Within months the church grew to around 100. For Grace this was rather small and she began planning for a much larger church. One reason for her desire to grow a large church was her hope that the new church would be planting other congregations in nearby communities very soon. She had already identified some potential leaders who might become future church planters.

Nearly everyone in Grace's church is West African, some are students at the nearby university but a good many are settled in Britain and planning to stay. A few members are from the West Indian community. With the exception of one person who is married to a Nigerian, there were no Anglo-Saxon English. That concerned Grace and she is already wondering how that might change. She is considering beginning a home group for Anglo people and wondering if her church could sponsor an Anglo church plant. For Grace, church planting has been hard work in the sense of much prayer, many hours of contacting people and spending time with them, planning and preparing. But her experience is also that growth flowed fairly easily from a receptive community. Not content with that growth she is also thinking about how to expand the work in terms of church plants and work among other ethnic groups.

Working in a neighbouring community

Jim was the assistant minister of a thriving suburban community church. The congregation was about ten years old and they were running out of space in the community centre in which they met. They had to make some choices. One possibility was to move to two morning worship services. They had plenty of people resource in terms of musicians and worship leaders. Adding another service was in one sense a 'no brainer'. However, they were aware that around seventy people were attending the church from a nearby community that was identical in terms of its social makeup but still geographically distinct.

Moreover, the leaders noticed that although they were able to attract existing Christians from this particular adjoining community, they had rarely or never been able to attract those who were not Christians. It was near enough for the committed to commute but too far to interest the curious but uncommitted. Jim was living in that adjoining area and although he had built many good relationships with unchurched people and even led some of them to a personal commitment to Christ, he realized that few if any would make the journey to church. In the case of those that he had led to faith, he had found it necessary to refer them to other local churches.

This process of questioning led the church to consider planting a congregation in the local area. Just as they were considering this possibility, they became aware that the local council was wanting to redevelop the local community centre. The existing community centre was old and too small for what had become a growing community. The council had access to funding, but experience with the existing centre had taught them that running a centre was far harder and more costly than building one. At that stage, a great deal of prayer took place and the general consensus seemed to be that God was opening a door for a new work.

Conversations with the council led the church to propose that they would run the centre to requirements laid down by the council. The church would take the financial risk of running the centre if they were permitted to hold worship services and other mid-week church meetings. The council agreed and nearly all of the seventy or so members who lived in that community became the founder members of the new church. Jim became the senior minister of the new church and sufficient growth took place swiftly that other staff members were appointed to help lead the work. The loss of the seventy members created some space in the mother church, and it was not too long before new people replaced those who had gone to the daughter church. That meant that the mother church was faced with their original problem of overcrowding and this time they decided to hold a second morning service.

An accidental plant

Mary was one of those women who everyone on the council estate seemed to know. Whenever there was a problem with a child, whenever someone had died, whenever a teenager went off the rails, or when marital problems loomed large, hers was the home that many other women on the estate made their way to. The teapot was never empty and seemed to last for ever. Mary's shoulders were broad and sympathetic. Her own marriage was good and Bill enjoyed the comfort that Mary brought to many, even though he never got involved in any direct sense. He liked to be supportive but in the background.

Then Mary became a Christian. It was the last thing that she had been expecting. Her mother had died and for once Mary was no longer in control, offering help to others. Now she needed comfort and solace. She found it in the rectory of the very sympathetic Rector who had taken the funeral service. More accurately it was the Rector's wife, Wendy, who had been on hand with the inevitable cup of tea and sympathy. The relationship between Wendy and Mary had led in time to Mary making a prayer of commitment and welcoming Christ into her life.

It was not difficult for Mary to share her new faith with people, partly because she was able to talk easily and freely to most people but also because so many of her neighbours, family and friends asked her to explain what it was that was so different about her. Before she fully realized what was happening a church had arisen in her home. She didn't describe it in that way for some time, she was only leading people to faith, taking Bible studies and teaching people some new songs. But after a time, many who were attending these regular meetings began telling others that a new church had started on the estate. Eventually they moved to a local community centre because the numbers had grown too large for any of the homes nearby.

Planting through healing meetings

Oliver is a Christian from central Africa who has lived and worked in Europe for a number of years. When he was in Africa, Oliver had been well known as a gifted evangelist. He had originally come to Europe to work with an international mission agency and was surprised by the decline of the church in Europe. He had heard of the weakness of the church but to experience it first-hand was new. Oliver and his wife, Naomi, had been wondering what contribution they might be able to make to mission in Europe beyond the work for their mission agency and membership of a local church.

They had made good friends with a number of Europeans who were very interested in spirituality but not in Christianity. Oliver and Naomi had gone with their friends to various psychic fairs and debated with a whole range of people involved in the New Age movement. That experience had led Oliver to a serious discussion with European Christians about how to engage with these New Age explorers. Eventually, and after much prayer and discussion, they decided to work with other helpers to attempt an experiment. The idea was to hold a healing crusade and advertise it heavily in ways that would connect with New Age information channels. Local Christians were contacted through the mission agency and other friends and enrolled to pray, distribute leaflets and help in a variety of practical ways.

The publicity emphasized that an African healer would be coming to town. Oliver knew from his days in Africa that prayer would be an essential key. He personally engaged in intercessory prayer and fasting for days before the event. He shut himself away in order that he might be fully open to God's voice. To the amazement of everyone involved, hundreds of people came to the meeting and the overwhelming majority were not Christians. Most had a New Age involvement and interest of some kind. A few were witches, others were astrologers, some were involved in New Age channelling and healing.

Astonishing events took place at the meeting. Oliver had prophetic words for many. These words revealed things about people that only God could have known. Some individuals began to shake, others fell to the ground. Oliver had seen this kind of phenomenon in Africa before but he had never seen middle-class Europeans behaving in such ways. More to the point, neither had Oliver's European helpers seen such things. Some who had been involved in witchcraft and other dubious practices were converted, and following a discipleship process a new church was launched. Was it really necessary to begin a new church? Would it not have been possible to send these converts to other existing local churches? It doesn't take much imagination to see that such converts would not fit easily in most existing churches and more particularly, it was easier for these converts to create spiritual settings conducive to reaching others from a New Age background.

Many who were converted were already experts at operating networks and informal organizations that dealt with spirituality. Beginning seeker-friendly churches was relatively easy for them once they had been well discipled. Since that time a number of other churches have been started using similar methods around public meetings.

Planting with a short-term team

Bill and Sharon were the two team members that I knew best and they, together with two other couples, were the long-term members of a much larger short-term team. The key idea was simply this. The six team members who were going to remain and lead the church longer term had all raised their long-term support from local churches that they knew well. They had spent nearly a year engaging in demographic studies to select the exact church location. In truth they had already decided on the city and the people group. They were intending to reach young professionals in a multicultural city. The church would therefore be English speaking but might contain nationals from many nations.

Having located the precise area and made connections with as many people as possible, the advance team drew together a number of young Christians who fitted the profile of those they were seeking to reach and who lived in the catchment area but who for various reasons were mostly not particularly committed to an existing local church. That group met together for some time and established a pattern of building large numbers of relationships with unchurched people with the same young professional profile.

While this was taking place, their mission organization had recruited a short-term international team, mainly of students who had finished their first degree and all of whom had good spoken English. They were asked to commit a minimum of three months. The team of fifty was then 'let loose', having been given a good briefing and many clues as to how to meet literally hundreds and eventually thousands of young professionals in that period of time. Those they met were invited to a myriad of social events, Bible studies, enquiry groups, and discussion encounters.

Towards the end of the three months, a public 'launch' service was held with contemporary music and a contemporary feel to the preaching, welcome, décor and indeed every aspect of the life of the emerging church. Literally hundreds came to the opening event and a couple of hundred stayed connected. Within a very short space of time, a large church with a distinctive mission focus was established. The short-term team mostly left during the two months that followed the conclusion of their minimum commitment. Some stayed longer and a few permanently. As the church developed, a good number of the new Christians are considering being part of planting teams elsewhere, some internationally. Some of these will be part of short-term teams but others will become permanent full-time church planters.

Planting by adoption

Times were looking bleak for the congregation at St Oswald's. The building, a late Victorian barn, was becoming increasingly difficult to maintain. Grass was growing where it should not grow – in the gutters and downpipes. Weeds were sprouting up in such profusion that a casual glance left one wondering if the building was in fact disused. It certainly seemed to lack care and attention. The congregation were rather elderly, far from wealthy and usually numbered less than twenty in a building that had seated 600 when it was opened. Some pews had been taken out to provide some other meeting space and the all important coffee point but even now it was far too large for the present worshippers. Closure was staring them in the face.

For many good reasons, the bishop was not anxious to close St Oswald's. Its geographic location was good, possibly even strategic, and there were reasons to think that the area was changing in ways that could be helpful to the gospel. The bishop wondered if it might be possible for the neighbouring St Luke's to lend a hand. In reality that meant a complete change of worship style, ministry style and leadership culture. St Luke's had a regular congregation close to 1,000 and after much discussion it was agreed to send Alan, one of their curates, and eighty other members to begin afresh at St Oswald's.

This fresh start was effectively a church plant into an existing building and the planning process was approached in this way. The question was asked, what will it take to reach every person in the catchment area? Interestingly, the new team did not use parish terminology as they thought of the evangelistic task. As part of the process, the building was significantly remodelled and made suitable for a more contemporary style of worship.

Thought was given to the provision of facilities for families, and additional staff members were recruited. Within a few months of the new start the congregation had grown to more than 200 and the first Alpha course was launched. Over 200 people were invited to the course and around 100 non-Christians actually attended. A pattern of growth that included a good deal of conversion growth was quickly established.

Reflecting on progress to date, Alan, the new vicar, paid tribute to the courage of those who had agreed to the transition. In one sense the future of their church had been guaranteed but they had had to give up much that had been treasured in the process. The fact that virtually all had stayed and become part of the new situation was cause for pleasure. Alan also paid tribute to the risk-taking on the part of the bishop. He had faced some criticism for the change of churchmanship, especially since he did not count himself as a card-carrying evangelical and that was the nature of the new culture.

These stories are all representative in nature. None of them refer to a single actual situation but in reality I could take you to several congregations that would easily fit most of the above descriptors. What does that tell us about the decision-making process in terms of determining where to plant a church? I would argue that the following factors all need to be present to some degree in terms of the decision to plant.

1. **Gifted people.** When I think of the many church planters I have met, I am well aware of the astonishing diversity in terms of personality, age, ethnicity, experience and social background. But I am also aware that they are all natural leaders who have an ease around

people, are naturally confident without being arrogant and who have a quiet determination to succeed. They are focused on the task and are not easily distracted from it. Most of the successful planters I have met have some evangelistic gifting. They are not necessarily just evangelists (though some have been) but at the very least they are able to share their faith naturally and easily. These are people who are personally secure and enjoy affirming others. They have not become planters because they found it difficult to minister elsewhere.

2. **Prayer and confirmation.** Very few planters that I have met have entered into commitments quickly. They have almost all been able to point to a long process of prayer, answers to prayer, questioning, more prayer, some confirmation and growing signs of being led to a particular path. The sense of journey therefore is very important. A number of planters have told me of some false starts that led up dead ends. They have had to stay remarkably open to changing circumstances and still be able to discern the voice of God through it all. That has usually kept them humble and yet confident in the guidance of God.

3. **Research around demographics.** This has usually played a part, though not in every case. Those who planted by accident tended not to work with any element of research, although even in these cases, once the work was established there was sometimes some later reflection on demographics as they asked themselves questions about how the work was likely to develop.

4. **An opportunity.** It might sound simplistic to say so but at some point an actual opportunity needs to present itself. All the demographic research available will not necessarily produce the opportunity. Equally, it can be a mistake to respond to an opportunity without giving it some thought in terms of its viability. I have

known numerous situations which looked like being an opportunity in terms of a building being available but which, on reflection, were not supported by the basic demographics of the situation.
5. **Creativity and passion.** Gifted leaders need to draw other gifted and passionate people around them. Successful church planting is rarely the consequence of one person and one person alone. In that sense, a church planter does need to be both a team player and a team creator. Their passion and creativity needs to be caught by a wider group or team in order for opportunities to be turned into a solid growing plant.

The way in which the various elements of gifted, creative and passionate leaders interact with opportunities and careful prayer and research is something of a mystery. It rarely follows a particular seven-step strategy. In that sense, church planting, as with leadership, is always more of an art than a science. There are few fixed boundaries even if there are some broad indicators.

Note
1. Robinson, Martin and Christine, Stuart, *Planting Tomorrow's Churches Today: A Comprehensive Handbook*, Monarch, 1992, chapters 7 and 9.

Chapter Four
The Gathering Process

Once a church planter or a church planting team have decided where they plant, attention shifts to the practicalities of getting started. That requires the gathering of an initial group of people with which to launch the church plant. Virtually all of the stories in the preceding chapter involve a gathering process of some kind. Sometimes, as in the case of St Oswald's, the gathering was easily accomplished because the initial group all came from a neighbouring church, in some other cases gathering came quickly because a large team was present. For many church plants the gathering process takes time and involves a good deal of entrepreneurial enterprise. Ed Stetzer comments:

> The most difficult phase of church planting may be the early stages, when the church planter is attempting to attract a core group of people. At this stage the planter can offer no relationships, no meeting place, no programs, and no music. People have difficulty committing themselves to a dream that they cannot see. Recruiting a core group is a challenging phase, but it is an essential stage in new church development. During this period, the planter lays the foundation for the birth of the new church.[1]

It is essential to note that the gathering process has a huge impact on the formation of the DNA of the church. The numbers being gathered operates in relationship to who is being gathered.

Let's deal first with the numbers issue. I have had some involvement in the planting of a number of churches, either as a sending minister or as a consultant of some kind. But I have only been directly involved as a church planter in planting one church. I recognize with the benefit of hindsight that I made some basic mistakes in that exercise. My key mistake was to begin with too small a group. How many should one seek to gather? The answer to that question depends on who you are seeking to reach. At this point we need to make a basic distinction between cross-cultural planting and planting that has little or no cross-cultural ingredient.

No cross-cultural ingredient

The majority of church plants take place using church planters who are not planting across cultures. In such cases I would suggest that the initial group that is gathered needs to be at least fifty strong before there is any kind of launch in a public worship setting. There are some purely practical reasons for this suggestion.

First, there is a social dynamic that means that newcomers feel somewhat exposed in a group that is smaller than fifty. A small group feels vulnerable and at least in a congregational setting for public worship feels like hard work. From a purely practical perspective the act of public worship needs a group that is significantly more than a large house group. Newcomers to a group that is significantly smaller than fifty people (for example thirty people) immediately sense that they can be known. Those who are already Christians might welcome being known but those who are not Christians, who are wanting to 'try on the clothes' before getting in too deep, desire some degree of anonymity. A warm welcome is one thing, experiencing a group that could fit into someone's home is another.

Second, from a financial perspective, the burden of renting worship space and possibly helping with a salary requires at least fifty people if it is not to become economically a strain. Third, it usually requires a group of at least fifty in order to locate the range of gifts needed to manage pastoral demands together with the preaching, evangelistic and worship requirements of a young church. The element of celebration, so important in public worship, requires a group of at least fifty people.

Experience suggests that groups that begin with less than fifty people find it difficult to grow. All too often the effort required to produce growth in a smaller group denudes the infant church of energy such that by the time a group of fifty is established exhaustion has already set in. Arriving at fifty can be such hard work if you launch too small that it feels as if you have arrived whereas it is actually just a starting point. It is far better to use energy to gather people than to use it to maintain a small group that has already gone public. Losing a family or two in a small group for the normal reasons that people move home can feel like a huge setback. Is there an upper limit for the size of a launch group? Not really. The only requirement is that the larger the group the more comprehensive the organizational structure needs to be prior to the actual launch.

That then leads to the question, what are the processes for identifying groups of fifty or more? There are three processes that can be utilized. The first is that the group is already identified from an existing source or set of sources. For example, a mother church sends out a large group or alternatively a group of churches act as joint sending churches and are jointly able to identify a ready-made group. Second, large numbers of potential members are located in a relatively short space of time by using activities such as large crusade meetings or by using a large initial team to make significant numbers of contacts quickly. These contacts then become the initial launch group.

Third, a smaller team works to establish evangelistic home groups that gather converts and disciples over a longer period of time prior to a public launch.

In all three of these processes it is vital to establish what we might call a multi-celled gathering. The core difference between a small church with little prospect of growth and an initial group of fifty with the potential to grow lies in whether it can be described as a single-cell or a multi-celled entity. Small churches are almost always single-cell structures.[2] In other words, all of the members of church know each other well and there is rarely more than one mid-week group meeting. The self-identity of the church is that of an extended family group. In multi-celled entities there are a number of mid-week groups and members only expect to know the members of their own group intimately. The self-identity of the multi-celled church is that of co-operating groups driving towards a single purpose rather than one group whose purpose is contained in simply being a single caring group.

The one outcome to avoid is to gather individuals in such a way that the primary gathering mechanism results in the attraction of Christians who are basically malcontents from other churches. Although there can be exceptions to this general rule, it is usually the case that bringing discontented members of other churches together is rather like herding cats – not impossible but contrary to nature! The experience of church planters is that churches planted with such an initial group rarely grow.

Cross-cultural intent

It is axiomatic that the process of gathering people to plant a church in a cross-cultural context requires that the initial church planting team be a relatively small group. The fundamental reason is that if the church planting team is too large then it becomes much more difficult to develop a group that becomes sensitive to the culture that is being reached. In effect the new converts from the target group are being asked to adopt the culture of the planting team. Although it is certainly possible to win some converts on this basis they will tend to be unrepresentative of the community and certainly not key influencers.

That almost certainly means that more time will need to be allowed for the initial gathering process to take place. If there are few existing Christians in the target community then by definition the members of the growing group will need to be new converts and it will take time to bring these converts through a discipleship process. That does not mean that the new church will grow slowly once momentum has been established but it does mean that great care needs to be taken in the initial gathering process.

That raises the question about the gifting of the initial planting team. Not everyone who is a leader of a growing church is a good initial gatherer of people. Many leaders need some existing people and structures in order to be able to lead. Those who can gather converts from no starting base at all are a rare breed but they do exist and need to be sought out if strong cross-cultural planting is to take place. It is not an inevitable rule but it is often the case that cross-cultural gatherers have themselves grown up in more than one culture. If pressed they are often unable to say which national group they most strongly identify with. They often see themselves as world citizens rather than citizens of a particular nation. I have often met gifted gatherers of people operating cross-culturally who turn out to be the children of missionaries who have grown up experiencing a number of different cultures.

Cultural exegesis

Good gathering requires those who are gathering to understand the culture of those they are seeking to reach. There was a time when church planting was thought of almost exclusively in terms of geographic communities. In recent decades, the concept of people groups defined in terms of ethnicity, age group or subculture has grown in importance for church planting. The work of Donald McGavran, among others, who interpreted Mathew 28 as reaching *ta ethnes* – all people groups, and not as it is more commonly translated, the whole world, has shifted attention to the importance of cultural exegesis.[3] Many writers, especially since the work of Ralph Winter, have noted the need to understand the Christian community as containing its own subculture. The distance between the culture of the worshipping community and broader Western culture has increased during the period of late modernity and early postmodernity.

Mark Driscoll, writing in *Radical Reformission*, makes the point very sharply:

> I am so hairy that I think I'm part Wookie. Consequently, I spend an inordinate percentage of my life shaving and sitting in a barber's chair for a haircut. Every time I get my hair cut, I undergo a cross-cultural experience. My barbershop is down the street from our church in an area known as the eccentric hangout for self-identified urban hipsters. Its claim to fame is an annual summer-solstice parade that features a nudist bicycling team. The barbershop is part of a small chain that promotes arty concerts and provides the finest selection of waiting-area pornography in our city.
>
> On one occasion, my young son Zac and I were getting our hair cut by a large flamboyant woman with bleached-blond hair, a black concert tank top, bright-red lipstick, jeans, and tattoos large enough to double as billboards. During the haircut, she fired a succession of questions at me about parenting that made me feel like a contestant on a game show. Near the end of the haircut, she thanked me for

my insight, told my son that he had a good daddy, and then informed us that she was going to be a good 'daddy' too.

Looking as if he had just taken a swig from a milk jug that was years past the expiration date, my son stared at me, wanting an explanation for how this woman could be a daddy. So I asked the woman if she was planning on getting pregnant. She said that she was not but that her girlfriend planned to conceive through a threesome with a male friend who liked to have sex with her and her 'wife'.

The woman could not have been nicer, yet she saw no difference between her marriage and mine, or my family and the one she was creating. Although we live in the same zip code, listen to the same music, and are roughly the same age, we live in very different cultures.[4]

We are now unequivocally missionaries in our own culture and although in one sense the church has always been a missionary community, there is a huge difference between a Western world whose social imagination was informed by the gospel and one which is largely ignorant of the gospel. As George Hunter has termed it, not a world full of agnostics but of ignostics. Most Christians have a huge amount of ground to cover in terms of exegeting the culture that is forming around us. It is an unfamiliar task and one that we need to learn quickly and well.

How do we go about such a task? No doubt there are those gifted individuals who are able to read the culture intuitively, but most of us are not instinctively able to engage in this task. Mark Driscoll offers some useful categories to help us down this path.

The first that he identifies is what he calls '**thought tribes**'. What he means by this is that we all carry a complex set of assumptions in our minds that act as filters through which we interpret information. This is not a conscious act and very few people are aware of the belief structure that informs our viewpoints. These deeply imbedded ideas operate to create what one sociologist has called 'plausibility structures'.[5] We judge whether an idea is likely to be true, whether it is plausible, not by a process of deep analysis from first principles, but by whether it sounds plausible against the structure of ideas that we already operate with and from.

Do we think it is likely that someone's account of being kidnapped by aliens is even worthy of consideration? Do we think that miracles can take place? How do we view alternative therapies? Do we think that angels exist and what would we think of those who claimed to have met one? How we do assess the concept of Karma or of Ying and Yang? In Western culture there is no longer a unified view about many ideas. Instead, there are 'thought tribes' each of which might form very different views about the plausibility of particular claims about truth.

Second, Driscoll talks about **'values tribes'**. In addition to ideas, we have deeply imbedded feelings about very complex systems, which again influence our response to, or feelings about particular claims or statements. The values we espouse are not always as obvious as the expression of ideas. Values go deeper and shape our response and assumptions in more hidden and yet very powerful ways. Value sets can often look very different from one another. Examples of values would be: freedom, independence, care for the poor, the importance of loving all, tolerance, the importance of tradition, the importance of family, the need for self-discipline, the importance of self-denial, loyalty to others (friends, family, tribe), truth-telling, openness, etc. The list could be very long indeed.

It does not take much imagination to see that a value set that speaks of the importance of family, tradition, loyalty to friends and the important of self-discipline could produce a very different attitude in relation to a value set that emphasizes freedom, tolerance and love for all. Values can clash in very dramatic ways. It is much more difficult to have a discussion about values as compared with ideas.

How have we received these values? Undoubtedly these were taught to us without us even realizing that we were breathing them in. Family, school but just as importantly, friends, and broader popular culture shape the assumptions. Those that we admire and love play a large part in shaping our value systems.

Third, Driscoll talks of '**experience tribes**'. The ideas and values that we have interact with our actual experience of the world. What was life like for us as we grew up? Moreover, as we experience the world, how does that shape our expectations? A good friend of mine, who happens to be happily married, was taken aback when his nine-year-old son came home from school one day and asked him, 'Daddy, when are you and mummy going to get divorced?' This was not a comment on their poor marital relationships but rather a reflection of the fact that all of the parents of his son's immediate circle of friends were divorced.

Experiences that involve trauma, illness, suffering, child abuse, alcoholism in the family, the death of a loved one, these and many other experiences combine to influence a person's outlook. When these experiences are commonplace in a community they begin to impinge heavily on the shape of culture in that locality. Subcultures that celebrate particular experiences or lifestyles emerge.

Fourth, Driscoll notes the difference between '**high culture**' and what he calls '**folk culture**' and '**pop culture**'. High culture would be things like ballet, opera and classical music. Driscoll helpfully points out that the elements of high culture all require discipline, time, patience and an awareness of an inheritance from the past. By contrast, folk culture is much more immediate and experienced at the level of the everyday. It is strongly related to communities. For Driscoll, pop culture is the city and a suburban, speeded-up version of folk culture. He points out that it is both more accessible and yet more fleeting and trite. It contains many fads that come and go quickly and feeds on personalities more than the quality of performance alone. For many people in the Western world, pop culture has replaced folk culture as a significant driver of fashion and a way of perceiving the world.

Driscoll is sceptical about the impact of high culture in shaping the present-day world. I am not quite so sceptical because many of those who have been involved in producing popular culture are themselves steeped in high culture. To listen to those who produce films and television programmes is to be introduced to people who know their Wittgenstein from their Sartre and their Plato from their Foucault. Watch the film *The Matrix* and then talk with the teenagers who have watched it and you know you are engaging with some very sophisticated ideas with young people who have no conception of the background of those ideas but are still being exposed to them.

Two questions now arise, how do we find out what ideas, values, experiences and influences people have from culture and how do we engage with that information to understand the world of those we are seeking to reach? Partly, we need to view the information we already have with a new awareness. To a large extent we are part of the same world or worlds as those we are seeking to reach; it is just that we have learnt to filter the information that comes to us somewhat differently. The reason for this is that consciously or unconsciously, we have a Christian framework of thought that provides us with a set of ideas, values and experiences that we use to evaluate the world around us. It is not that we should abandon those ideas so much as we need to enter imaginatively the world of those who do not share our Christian horizon.

A good place to begin is a news-stand. What are people buying and reading in your community? What does it tell you about their pastimes, pleasures, hobbies and ideas? Not too long ago I was visiting a friend in a large American city. We had a morning together to just hang out. I asked my friend what he would like to do. He is an avid reader and loves theology. I suppose I knew what he was going to say and sure enough it came, 'There is a great bookshop near us that serves good coffee and has a huge Christian section. Why don't we go down there and we can look at some of the latest books over coffee and muffins?' I was proud of his increased sensitivity – he knew I liked great coffee. I agreed but on one condition – we would also look at the news-stand and he would help me to exegete what we found.

It was a wonderful morning. We found magazines that looked at the relationship between fashion (in the sense of clothes) and furniture, dozens on spirituality of various kinds, hunting, fishing, guns, needlepoint and many more. It was bewildering and bizarre as well as deeply impressive in its own way. What had we learnt? At the very least we were looking at an astonishingly diverse community that had a very independent streak and a growing interest in exploring spiritual issues. We sat and talked about the experience and realized that these days we very rarely engaged in cultural exegesis. We resolved to do better!

Of course there are many ways of engaging with the ideas of those who live around us. The news-stand can be a fun place to begin but simply listening more attentively to conversations, to the radio, television and film, by reflecting more carefully on the lifestyles of those around us, how they spend their money, the relationships they form, and the causes they pick up, we gradually begin to gain a sense of what matters to these people, of how they think and act. Those who are engaging in the gathering process for church planting need to be good practitioners of cultural exegesis. Some will do it intuitively and others, like me, need to work at it a little harder. As the church planting group continues to form and the numbers grow prior to launch it will also be essential to ensure that cultural exegesis continues. Building in an awareness of the culture of those that we are seeking to reach contributes towards building the right missional DNA and helps to prevent the growth of a Christian subculture that is resistant to the outside world.

We need to be clear what we are doing in this process. This is not a marketing exercise that is a prelude to shaping our message so that it is accessible to our consumer market. The gospel will always contain two contrasting elements. On the one hand it really is good news. Because it is a message about reconciliation with God, our heavenly Father, there is always a sense of coming home, of joy, peace of fulfilment. The ultimate reality of the universe is a foundation of love because God is love. The problem is that many in the cultures that we are seeking to reach have a variety of aspirations, not all of which are in accord with the gospel. The point about cultural exegesis is that we need to learn how to connect with the good parts of the longing of the human heart.

The second contrasting element flows from what we have just noted above, namely, that no matter what the culture we are dealing with there is always a counter-cultural element in the gospel. There will always be a dimension that is foolishness to the Greeks and a stumbling block to the Jews. It is not always natural to count others better than ourselves, to seek to live as a servant or to love without counting the cost. But no matter how great the essential counter-cultural element of the gospel, it is vital that we do not add to that aspect by adding barriers and burdens that are really unrelated to the gospel. The Christian faith is able to express itself in many cultural clothes and still remain the gospel.

People of peace

As we engage in the process of cultural exegesis, we also need to be on the lookout for 'people of peace'. They, more than any other people, will be able to naturally interpret the gospel in and to the culture that we seek to reach. The use of the term 'people of peace' has been used extensively by church planters around the world and is based on the scripture in Luke 10:5–12 where Jesus issues his instructions to the seventy-two that he sends on a mission. He instructs them to look for 'a man of peace' and then to build their mission on that home. These people of peace are well connected to the communities in which they live. They provide keys of trust to many who live around them.[6] Let me describe four such people. Once again, names and some of the details have been changed but these examples are based on real people and situations.

In the first church in which I ministered in inner-city Birmingham, England, we conducted door-to-door evangelistic calling. The intention was to find homes in which we might hold discussion groups based on an enquiry into the Christian faith. We had not called on more than a few homes before we found a very ready welcome. Not only were there occupants more than ready to hold such a meeting, they also insisted that they would recruit the participants. The key person was Rachel who was a kind of mother to the neighbourhood. Anyone in trouble tended to find their way to Rachel's door.

Rachel was as good as her word and a lively group began meeting in her home. After some weeks, at the end of the study, a number of people made commitments and were subsequently baptized. Rachel was not one of these but she continued to make good connections for us into the neighbourhood, developing extensive relationships of trust on our behalf. In addition to building bridges she also offered a fascinating insight into the values and views of those who lived in the area. Eventually Rachel herself came to faith and was baptized.

The converts that came through Rachel's good offices were the very first converts that this particular church had seen for many years. More particularly, they were the only converts from the immediate estate in which the church was set. Prior to this process the church in question had been attempting to replant itself in the community and until making contact with Rachel had been spectacularly unsuccessful in making any inroads into the community at all.

Rachel and that initial group of converts were taken through an extensive discipleship process, some of which was led by one or two leaders in the church who were not involved in the original discussion group. The impact on the church leaders was just as important as the impact on the new converts. Through these discipleship debates, all held in homes and not in the church building, the church leadership began to read the community differently. Small but significant changes took place in the worship style, the pastoral approach and the attitudes of many in the church. The conduit provided by this first person of peace proved to be foundational in a gradual shift of culture in that local church.

Another church that I came to know recently was a new church plant that had grown fairly effectively and as a consequence of their growth was considering a move to another location. They had been hiring a local community hall and they had outgrown the facility. A decision was made to explore another venue and as part of that process the leadership spent some time with a key decision-maker whose permission was required in order for the move to be made. We will call him Keith. Keith was not a Christian and had never really had any significant contact with Christians prior to this set of conversations.

He had many questions, most of which were designed to help him understand the motivation of the church. What were they trying to do? What kind of church was it? What were their objectives and values? The church in question had a particular emphasis on youth and sought to provide programmes of a sporting nature for young people as a way of building relationships with un-churched youth. As time went by, Keith began to get a feel for the intentions and heart of the church.

Eventually Keith became an advocate for the church and made an astonishing promise. He indicated that if the church moved to the new location, he would ensure that the church would grow. As far as the church was concerned that was a rather surprising statement. Keith was not a Christian, it was by no means clear that he was planning to attend himself. What did he mean by indicating that he would help the church to grow? It became clear that what he meant was this, he would use his extensive network of connections to speak well of the church and he would encourage people to come.

His network of connections was not related to youth but he felt that he had understood the values of the church and he could identify the kind of people who would share that value system, even though none of the people he had in mind were Christians either. Keith's claims have yet to be tested because the move has not yet been made, but even at this early stage, many conversations have begun. A large network of people have been identified that previously the church has never been able to reach.

A third situation relates to a church which had been in existence for some time but which had not seen any significant growth for some time. A new minister with strong evangelistic gifts came to the church and he had the ability to make connections with people in the immediate community. Some small amount of progress was made but nothing that made a huge amount of difference to the situation. The church was still small, rather inwardly focused and not really connected to the community.

There then came a single conversion that was to change all that. The details are not important but what made a huge difference was that this particular convert, we will call him Jim, had a huge network of family and friends.

Jim ran a small family business and his rather dramatic conversion and subsequent change of lifestyle immediately attracted attention through his natural network. Within an eighteen-month period around seventy-five people were added to the church, all of whom were related to Jim in some way or another. The church was suddenly nearly three times the size it had been.

The growth of the church not only impacted the lives of a whole network of new Christians, it also changed the way in which the church operated. Almost overnight the culture of the church was changed. The subsequent change in the ability of the church to understand those they were seeking to reach allowed the church to grow well beyond that initial network. Within five years, the church had grown to around 400 people and it became a congregation that planted a number of other churches in surrounding areas.

A rather different situation arose in another community through the personal witness of a Christian couple. We will call them Andrew and Jenny. They were members of a local church and over the years they had been effective personal evangelists. They had led many people to faith and a good percentage of these individuals began to attend the local church that Andrew and Jenny belonged to.

Recently they came to meet a new neighbour who had just moved to a home nearby. She was a Muslim woman, in her middle years, who had moved home because of her recent divorce. Andrew and Jenny built a good relationship with her and in time she expressed interest in the Christian faith.

It was at this point that Andrew and Jenny made a difficult but imaginative decision. They realized that Aisha had an extensive set of connections with other Muslims in the wider area and they began to wonder how wise it might be to invite her to their local church. There were many reasons for their questions but the most important was the realization that even if Aisha could make the transition to their very Anglo-Saxon local church, it was very unlikely that many of her contacts could. Instead, they have been working with Aisha to create a home group that features discussion around what it means to remain culturally Muslim but become followers of Jesus. The intention is to build a home group of Jesus followers that could be replicated in other homes.

Once again, it is too early to say what might happen in this particular situation but it is clear that the connection with people of peace needs to be looked at very sensitively. Two principles might be drawn out of these stories. First, it can sometimes block the effectiveness of a person of peace to remove them from their circle of influence and transfer them to the church too quickly. They are people of peace in their own situation and they can all too easily cease to be people of peace if they are removed from their cultural context. The move to some churches can be a bridge too far, a journey that causes the bridge to collapse. It can be more effective to build new communities around people of peace rather than ask them to leave their natural network and join what can sometimes be the culturally inappropriate setting of an existing church.

Second, people of peace are not just bridges to a new network of contacts, they are also interpreters of the culture to be reached. If, as a new church is being formed, the culture of the community that people of peace allow to be accessed can be well understood such that the developing church can take on the clothes of that culture, then people of peace can help to define the culture of the group that is being gathered.

Notes
1. Stetzer, Ed, *Planting New Churches in a Postmodern Age*, Broadman and Holman Publishers, 2003. p. 203.
2. For more on the relationship between single celled make-up and small churches see, Robinson, Martin and Yarnell, Dan, *Celebrating the Small Church*, Monarch, 1993.

3. McGavran, Donald, *Understanding Church Growth*, Eerdmans, 1970.
4. Driscoll, Mark, *The Radical Reformission: Reaching Out Without Selling Out*, Zondervan, 2004, p. 91f.
5. The concept of plausibility structures for belief was first used by the sociologist Peter Berger and was then used by Newbigin, Lesslie in *The Gospel in a Pluralist Society*, SPCK, 1989.
6. David Garrison, sees the "Person of Peace" as a key in the development of church planting movements. He writes: "Several of the Church Planting Movements we've examined attest to the missionary method of sending church planters into villages in search of God's "person of peace," that individual already chosen by God to receive the gospel message. Their motivation is to adhere to the model established by Jesus. When Jesus first dispatched his disciples as missionaries, he sent them out two-by-two and commanded them to enter every village in search of the "man of peace" who would welcome them and their message." Garrison, David, *Church Planting Movements: How God is Redeeming a Lost World*, WIGTake Resources, 2004, p. 211.

Chapter Five
Building the Team

As the gathering process take place, it soon becomes clear that the success or otherwise of a new church plant does not depend on a single individual, no matter how gifted a particular leader might be. Church planting is first and foremost a team effort. In this chapter we will look at two key issues, who is in the team and how does the team function?

Before we go too far, we need to be clear which team we are describing. Churches, indeed any organization, have a number of teams within them. In this chapter we are talking about the primary leadership team. That might be entirely composed of full-time church planters but more likely it will be a mixture of full-time or part-time trained leaders and significant lay leaders. What happens within this team will set the tone for every other team in the church. More than any other group of people, this team helps to create and sustain the culture of the church that is being planted. If a strong missional DNA is to be present, it will be this team that has a primary responsibility for generating and sustaining it.

A number of books on church planting make the biblical case for working in teams. Partly because the case is already so well made I do not intend to cover this ground. Suffice it to say that the biblical case is grounded in four key areas: God's nature as Trinity suggests team. Jesus established a team. The various images of the church in the New Testament, for example the body and the stones of a temple, all point to team and at a practical level Paul created a church planting team with close to thirty people actually mentioned in the New Testament. The notion of team is no longer a revolutionary idea and does not require an elaborate apologetic. We seem to have accepted the concept of teams over and against the model of the single leader, but that does not necessarily mean that we know how to make teams work.

Putting spice into the team

If variety is the spice of life, then a variety or difference of giftedness certainly puts spice into team. Difference is the strength of team but it is also its vulnerability. It is vitally important for team members to understand each other well and to know the needs of the various team members in terms of communication. Of course, some teams will be composed of those who are already friends and who have a good intuitive understanding of each other. Even in these cases, working together imposes strains on friendship that need to be understood and anticipated to some degree. How can one do that?

One approach is to use one or other of the various psychometric tools that are available for team building. Using these tools is not a substitute for hard work, far from it. Engaging in the process of using psychometric tools demands a degree of persistence and commitment to the task. These tools never provide ready-made solutions but they do offer a framework through which hard work can produce significant results. At the very least, it is vital to know how each team member communicates and what they need in terms of communication to be able to operate effectively.

Probably the best known psychometric tool available is

Myers Briggs. As a tool it has the advantage that more research and development has been undertaken on this tool than many others. The concepts are widely understood and relatively easy to access. In particular there is a good amount of literature available on the use of Myers Briggs in relation to teams.

In addition to psychometric tools which have the disadvantage of being rather generalized in their presentation of 'types' there are also some tools which begin from the perspective that every individual is entirely unique and cannot easily be contained or understood within a 'type'. The System for Identifying Motivated Abilities (SIMA) is one of the more sophisticated and available approaches in terms of locating individual patterns of personal motivation.

It must be emphasized that team members should not be recruited with reference to psychometric types. That represents a misuse of these tools. Rather, these tools should be used to aid understanding within the team. Myers Briggs uses a variety of contrasting polarities as a means of understanding personal preferences. One such polarity is that of 'Extrovert' or 'E's' and 'Introverts' or 'I's'. The needs and preferences of these different kinds of people are very different. The 'E' talks a problem through whereas the 'I' is more likely to reflect on the problem internally before verbalizing their conclusion.

One happily married couple I know, who have been married more than thirty years, were reflecting with a small group of friends around the meal table on the early years of their marriage. The husband happened to be a marked 'I' and the wife a rather strong 'E'. As the evening progressed and the courses of food continued, they spoke of a crisis that occurred after six months of marriage. The wife told her then new husband, 'We are in real trouble, I think this marriage is over.' The husband responded, 'What are you talking about, I've never been happier?' 'But,' remonstrated his wife, 'I never know what you are thinking.' The husband was astonished and replied, 'But I tell you everything I think you need to know.' It's hard work for Es and Is to figure out the communication process but the rewards are worth the effort.

Gifts within the team

What gifts need to be present in a church planting team in order for it to be effective? In recent years, much has been written about the pattern of ministry gifts alluded to in Ephesians chapter 4, namely apostles, prophets, evangelists, pastors and teachers. Most writers see these ministries as a functional description of team gifts rather than positions of authority or hierarchy. Somehow, in the general mix of a church planting leadership team, these gifts need to be present in order for the new plant to function healthily.

In very broad terms we can think of the first three gifts (apostle, prophet and evangelist) as containing a strong entrepreneurial thrust and the second two gifts (pastor and teachers) as containing an element of support and maintenance. Many leaders will have a combination of these gifts and it is important to have a strong understanding within the team of the nature and contribution of each team member's gifts. It is possible that some of these gifts may be absent from a church planting team. If that is so, then the plant could be significantly weakened in some important respect. Certainly the absence of one of these gifts in the leadership team needs to be compensated for in some way. Is it possible to find someone from outside the emerging team, perhaps based in another church to provide some short-term help? In the area of pastoral care and/or teaching, is it possible to develop a number of people in the emerging group that is being gathered to contribute this element?

A good team will also have access to a number of other gifts. My colleague and co-writer, Dwight Smith, speaks of four additional gifts each of which have management outcomes:

- Administration – the management of detail
- Organization – the management of structure
- Management – the management of people
- Leading – the management of the future

How do these four management areas relate to the five ministry gifts from Ephesians? Clearly, the management of the future is strongly related to the apostolic gift and the management of people to the pastoral gift, but the other two management areas might not be present within the team orientated around the five-fold listing from Ephesians and yet are very valuable in terms of team effectiveness. These gifts do not have to be in the primary team but the primary team must have a strong relationship with people who do have these gifts. The primary team can be thought of as an eldership and the team who implements in terms of a deaconate.

The difficulty with such language is that it has an ecclesial significance that is not intended in a purely functional description of teams in relation to leadership. Dwight Smith has a useful visual analogy when he places the fingers of one hand into the fingers of his other hand. The five ministries of Ephesians are knitted into the four functions of management such that they support and help one another.

The nature of teams

The literature on teams reveals that individuals have many different understandings of the nature of a team. Some teams are in reality task groups, others are think tanks while still others have no work component but seek to mutually support those in the team from a pastoral perspective. A church planting leadership team must have at least two key elements. There must be some accountable work output and there must be a strong element of mutual support and friendship. With this in mind I would suggest that a good definition of team can be found in the work of Katzenbach and Smith: 'A small number of people with complementary skills who are equally committed to a common purpose, goal, and working approach for which they hold themselves mutually accountable.'[1]

It is helpful to dissect the elements of Katzenbach and Smith's definition.

'A small number of people....' If there are too few in the team, it is inadequately resourced. If there are too many, there can be too many opinions so it will take too long to work through issues as everyone gets 'air time' in the discussions. A large team can become unworkable. Somewhere from five to seven members seems to work well.

'Complementary skills....' A team of seven people with six administrators and a pastoral type will not achieve much – but what they do achieve will be undertaken in a highly efficient manner and with lots of tender loving care! A team with five visionaries, one administrator and one reflective type may explode in a cloud of glorious vision; the administrator will burn out and the reflective type will end up in therapy for some considerable time! Gifts and skills need to be balanced against the mission and vision, with a reasonable distribution of key skills.

'Equally committed...'. This ensures that everyone pulls together in harness with no one doing more than they ought, no one doing less than they ought.

'A common purpose, goal...'. This ensures that the team is working toward the same ends, and a sense of cohesion comes to the working environment.

'Working approach...'. This ensures they share a common philosophy of ministry, meaning that agreement will be reached on values, methods and strategy, enabling true synergy to take place.

'Willing to hold themselves mutually accountable...'.

This ensures the high performance of the team. Ministry is one of those jobs where it is possible to 'hide' somewhat behind spiritual reasons for not getting the job done. In a real team, performance is measured against mutually agreed individual and team goals set in terms of a realistic but challenging time frame.

This is what we want to call a real team. It is not a short-term task force, or a church board or working group, it has the dynamic of commitment to mission, accountability and mutuality of ministry that is in evidence anywhere you see a healthy church sustaining long-term results. The truth is many of us have been in teams with a lack of clear purpose and no real team philosophy or values. The outcomes of such teams are usually disappointing.

If our experience of church teams is that they fail to perform effectively, what are the characteristics of more effective teams? Ken Blanchard and E. Parise-Carew list the characteristics of great teams, using the acrostic P.E.R.F.O.R.M.:

Perform. These teams have:
- Purpose and shared values
- Empowerment – every member has authority commensurate with their responsibilities
- Relationships and communication are open and honest
- Flexibility, so that structures and guidelines facilitate the work rather than hinder it
- Optimal productivity – there is a high level of output because there is an effective means of making decisions and solving problems
- Recognition and appreciation – so that members who achieve goals are rewarded and affirmed for their excellent performance
- Morale is high because of the above and the creative and fun environment the leader establishes.[2]

Team processes

So far we have spent some time examining who should be in a team from the perspective of gifts and abilities and the related characteristics of good teams. We now need to turn to the equally important issue of how a team functions. The literature on team process is legion and there can be a danger that if a team spends too much time gazing inwardly in an attempt to identify the perfect team process, that little work will be done. It is essential therefore to strike a balance between a healthy process that involves self-knowledge on the part of the team and constructive work output.

One suggestion in relation to group process is to use an external facilitator from time to time who is skilled in group process. Many teams who have encouraged individual team members to use the already mentioned Myers Briggs typing, use the same tool to increase team awareness in relation to group process.

The balance between healthy process and work output is helped by ensuring that the team has a mutual commitment to an agreed framework of aims and objectives. It is wise to use that agreement as a template to check progress at least once a year but more likely two or three times a year. A common template features the headings Purpose, Vision, Values and Goals.

Purpose

The leadership expert John Adair once wrote: 'The first commandment in any institution, organization or working community is to be clear about its purpose. Once purpose is seen clearly and agreed upon then other things tend to fall into place.'[3]

It is vital for a church plant to be clear about its purpose before it begins. The larger the church grows the more difficult it will be to sustain that original purpose. The arrival of families with children produces a demand to offer programmes for those children. The same will be true for the singles, the young adults, the seniors and many other groups with particular interests. Fellowship is often cited as a valid Christian motivation for organizing many adult groups. It is hard to be against fellowship but it can easily represent a slippery slope towards the inversion of the church such that its own members' needs take priority over the key purpose of the church.

So what is the purpose of the church? *To proclaim the gospel and to offer a living demonstration of the gospel such that the world is reconciled to God and human beings are reconciled to one another.* That is not a mission statement as such but the mission statements of most churches reflect the contents of that statement in one way or another. The task of leadership is to be clear about the purpose of the church, to ensure that the purpose of the church is acted on in the life of the church and to resist activities that undermine the purpose of the church.

Vision

Having gained a sense of what the church is for and what its nature should be like it is necessary to move on to the next step and describe in contextual terms what the nature and purpose of the church will look like in a given community. What will be the priorities in the foreseeable future? *If you could sit down and draw a picture of what the church would feel like and look like in five or ten years' time that the leadership and the majority of the church could agree on, what would that picture be?*

In particular, would that picture, or vision, truly reflect the purpose and nature statements already agreed on, or is that vision reflecting a community that once again is being drawn towards meeting its own needs? A missional church ensures that its vision is consistent with the missional nature and purpose of the church.

Values

If the purpose of the church is to proclaim and demonstrate the reconciling love of God then the nature of the church is to create the kind of community in which outrageous grace is lived out. People ought to be able to see the values of grace acted out in the kind of community that is created by the gospel. The church of the first few centuries was noted as the kind of community where the poor, the marginalized and the powerless were cared for. Ministry to those in prisons has long been a feature of Christianity precisely because prisoners were all of these things. Gibbons, in his lament over the decline and fall of the Roman Empire, blames Christianity for weakening the cruelty, harshness and will of Rome. In some senses Gibbons was correct. Christians should be proud to plead guilty to such a charge.

It therefore should be possible to see Christian communities in which people develop better relationships within families and among each other as friends. Leaders in particular will be noted for the way in which they deal with conflict. It is not that conflict can be avoided but more that tension and disagreement should become a catalyst for relational health and growth rather than for division and broken relationships.

Goals

Goal-setting needs to be undertaken in relation to the vision. The vision and values of a church are sometimes rather soft in terms of presenting something of the flavour of what the church will look like. Somewhere between vision and goals, a harder edge needs to be present. That harder edge can be unearthed by beginning to ask some questions about the exact shape of the mission of the church. In terms of the vision that has been painted, for whom or for what is the church ready to be accountable?

All too often when you ask a church or a leadership

team who they are trying to reach or serve, the reply will come 'everyone'. That can sometimes be followed by a slightly more thoughtful, 'everyone who could reasonably get to us'. But who could reasonably get to you and are you really wanting to shape your ministry such that it reaches such a widespread community? In reality we are not trying to reach everyone. Even if we are attempting to reach a group that is not strictly geographically defined but is defined by factors such as ethnicity, or age or socio-economics, there are always some geographical limitations. The failure to be clear about who we are trying to reach prevents us from accepting clear accountability. It stops us from constructing some kind of framework for knowing where we are going and what we should be doing. In short, we cannot set goals in an accountability vacuum.

That is why we must be certain that we know who we are accountable for. It is very possible that we cannot be responsible for touching the lives of everyone in a given community, not just because there may be too many people for us to connect with. It is also likely that we are best positioned to reach a particular age group or socio-economic group. When we really think about who we might realistically connect with we might find that we can define that group very clearly. We cannot be held accountable for those that we have little opportunity of reaching and to do so might jeopardize our efforts to reach those that we do have the possibility of connecting with. *It is important to be focused in our efforts while being open to the possibility that God the Holy Spirit might dramatically intervene to offer us completely unexpected opportunities.*

Part of the reason that we should be realistic about who we are attempting to reach relates to the question, who else should we partner with? What other churches in the local area, town or city could help us complete the task? Another version of the same question is to ask, what other resources do we need to help us reach those for whom we cannot presently be accountable for but who fall within the remit of our broader vision? What other organizations can help us with resources for the task we face?

A great deal of team building takes place as we engage in the process of coming to answers about Purpose, Vision, Values and Goals. The team that has worked through these questions and returns to them as a check against progress is a very different team from the one that has not grappled with this task.

Along the way, there will be informal as well as formal processes that help to engender a sense of a joyful team. Those processes will be greatly helped if team members, especially the team leader, can contribute the following qualitative ingredients. These are behaviours which need to be present in the leadership team. You might want to ask yourself how your team performs in relation to these behaviours.

Key team qualities and behaviours

Confidence and hope
The leadership team are the people to whom others automatically turn to for encouragement and inspiration. The team sets the tone for an organization – if the team looks uncertain then the whole church becomes worried. This is a key ingredient particularly in the process of change. People are easily unsettled by the loss of the familiar and by the blazing of new trails. The confidence of the team in their vision and strategy that they have worked on together with their positive attitude rights the ship and restores confidence when the church plant encounters problems.

Setting an appropriate pace
The pace of the leadership team sets the standard for the whole church. The problem is rarely a lack of pace. Most leaders get the organization moving because of their

energy and enthusiasm. The problem is most likely to be setting an unsustainable pace for the team and hence for the whole church. Drop-out through burnout can result.

One leader offers this testimony:

> After some years in my ministry, I asked the staff to journal the amount of hours and tasks they were involved in. To my surprise, they were all up around 55–60 hours a week, and involved in too many projects. I found I was up to about 60 hours and couldn't see a way of getting them down. I had set a burnout pace. We took that process as a significant learning point, and developed job-descriptions and boundaries around them that took into account family time and the need for renewal.

Persistence and constancy

Many have noted that success is 1 per cent inspiration and 99 per cent perspiration. There will be times when the team will be sorely tempted to buckle under pressures or discouragement, but if the team is on the right track, pursuing the mission and vision, it can be more vital to 'hang in there' than to introduce new strategies. The Duke of Wellington is reputed to have responded to the question as to why his armies were so successful by noting that 'they fight about five minutes longer than other soldiers'. Leaders don't give up. They may need to change tack, or eventually try a new approach, but when God gives leaders a vision, they keep on going until they see it coming to pass.

Leadership teams give a great gift to the church when it is clear that they are faithfully pursuing the mission. It adds tremendously to their sense of the value of the mission when people see persistence and determination. Conversely, when a team or a church sees their leaders dropping projects and coming up with new visions when the going gets tough, the result can be a growing demotivation. Consistency over time counts for a great deal.

Asking the right questions
Some in leadership labour under the misapprehension that leaders have to have all the right answers. In reality you can lead a lot more effectively if you ask the right questions. In some ways this flies in the face of the image of the strong leader, who is able to develop and drive a vision almost on the strength of his or her own talents. But actually, it is a strategy more and more leaders are using not only to discover possibilities and direct their thinking, but also to build ownership within their teams of the vision and tasks ahead. So, what are the right questions? Robert Banks, formerly the Director of the Dupree Leadership Institute, offers this very helpful outline on the role of questions in developing vision and strategy.

The *perception* question is simply 'what's going on here?' The leader's attitude here is of patient inquisitiveness. The leader asks the questions that help the team understand the reality of their current situation.

The *making* question is simply 'what shall we do?' The leader fosters an inventive, can-do sense in the team that focuses on the pathways, not just the blockages. The leader may provoke by asking why can't we? Why not? Is there another way? What levers can we pull?

The *art* question is simply 'How?' What methods, what processes, what initiatives need to be developed in order to make progress? Have we got the resources or where can we get them from? Who will do what?

The *will* question is surprisingly important: What will come of this? Out of this question spring images of the new vision, developing dreams together in ways like this builds very high levels of commitment and energy for the work ahead. Next time you want to make a forward move in the ministry, refrain from telling people what you think, but instead invite the group into a discovery process that values their input. You still lead, but instead of leading from the front, you lead from within the group.

Keeping commitments – credibility
If your people discover that the team doesn't keep their commitments, then credibility with the leadership team together with its influence will vanish. That particularly applies to the team leader. If you have ever been on a team where the leader cancels meetings, individual and team, you will know the sense of frustration that causes. If leaders say they will phone or visit someone, and don't, the message they send is that people are not valued. If leaders say that they are launching a new ministry on a certain date, and it keeps getting put further and further back, the perception will be either that they are incompetent or untrustworthy. Better not to make a commitment and give others a pleasant surprise, than to make one and fail to keep it.

If a team consistently displays the behaviours that we have outlined above then there is a strong possibility you have a great team. The creation and sustaining of a good team is a great achievement. However, there are some tasks that belong primarily to the team leader. The team leader will stand a better chance of creating a great team if they keep their eye on the following critical team leader checklist.

Key tasks for a team leader

Define reality
Team leaders are able to see through the woolly thinking and spiritualization of the current situation, and bring a realistic assessment of how things actually are. Most churches are happily plateaued and have started the death roll long before anyone realizes it. Many of the inner-city churches around the Western world either disappeared or were reduced to the faithful few octogenarians who had been part of that church since they were children. Why? Because no one could see the new reality of multi-culturalism even

as tens of thousands of non-English speaking migrants flooded their suburbs. We live in the new reality of a post-modern, post-Christian mindset in the people we try to reach, yet the average sermon is still a three pointer with a poem at the end! The mission church movement is confronting the new reality with 180° shift from attracting people to our spaces to developing relationships with people in their spaces.

See the future
Team leaders have the gift of seeing the future in such a way as to make it a present reality in their own minds. For these leaders, the question is not 'will the vision become reality?' It is simply a question of when. This isn't very often a mystical vision appearing in a dream. Most often it is a realization or revelation coming after many, many hours of prayer and research, probing and questioning the future. Nevertheless, no matter how it comes, these leaders develop such a clear picture of it they have little trouble explaining it to others and getting their buy-in.

Build the team
Team leaders recognise that the future cannot be built apart from the creation of a team that will enable it to come to fruition. The building of a team becomes a top priority because only in team will there be sufficient gifts, creativity, time and resource to enable the vision to be brought to reality. Seeing that reality and creating the team are of course two very different exercises.

One of the weaknesses of gifted leaders with a strong sense of future vision is that they do not always have sufficient people skills to build the team. They tend to live too much in the future and not pay enough attention to the present. The domination of the future can become an intimidating factor for other team members. Team leaders therefore need to be realistic enough to know that they must have others in the team who can contribute people skills in order to make the team a happy place.

Communicate the vision

Team leaders need to be able to cast vision. Through stories, preaching, statements, every kind of publication and at every meeting, the vision is stated and restated as many ways as possible. This is due partly because Team leaders are so excited about the vision and partly because they know you have to keep the vision in front of people constantly to keep them moving forward.

Develop and guard the culture

The culture a church or ministry develops over time in itself provides leadership to the group. For example it becomes normal for people to share their faith with friends in a church where there are constant stories of people doing that, and people come to faith regularly. In churches where that doesn't happen, it becomes normative for people not to share their faith.

The team leader must find ways to inculcate the cultural values that the team is adopting.

If you are seeking to lead a great team and you consistently do well with the above tasks, you should not have too much difficulty in recruiting team members. However, it is vital to remember that being a member of the team needs to be good fun. It is not all about the task, it is just as much about playing as working. Just recently I was with a team whose team leader made a virtue of always being on time and he expected others on the team to be punctual. His saying was 'If you are early, you are on time. If you are on time, you are late, if you are late, it is unacceptable."

As they were explaining this to me, one team member told me that on one occasion their team leader had locked the door so that latecomers knew they were late. At that precise moment the team realised that their team leader was absent and that we were due to begin our meeting. Quick as a flash they locked the door! This was a team that knew how to have some fun as well as work hard.

Daniel Goleman calls this 'emotional intelligence'. He writes extensively of the importance of 'playfulness' in the tool kit of emotionally intelligent leaders. He particularly alludes to the importance of laughter and the 'shortest distance between two people'. He goes on to explain that 'people who relish each other's company laugh easily and often; those who distrust or dislike each other, or who are otherwise at odds, laugh little together.' In describing emotionally intelligent leaders he is not only talking about leadership in general but he is giving a good summary of the kind of leadership that healthy church planting teams need. He continues with this telling comment, very pertinent to the creation of high performing teams:

> Leaders with that kind of talent are emotional magnets; people naturally gravitate to them ... It's one reason emotionally intelligent leaders attract talented people – for the pleasure of working in their presence.[4]

Remember, great teams also have fun together.

Notes
1. Katzenbach, Jon R, and Smith, Douglas K, *Wisdom of Teams: Creating the High Performance Organization*, McKinsey, 1993
2. Blanchard, Ken and Parise-Carew, Eunice, *The One Minute Manager Builds High Performance Teams*, Harper-Collins, London, 1992.
3. Adair, John, *Creative Church Leadership*, Canterbury Press, 2004, p. 13.
4. Goleman, Daniel, Boyatzis, Richard and McKee, Annie, *The New Leaders: Transforming the Art of Leadership in the Science of Results*, Little, Brown, 2002, p. 11.

Chapter Six
Discipleship and the Creation of Community

The church in the West has placed a great deal of emphasis on the issue of evangelism throughout the modern period. Whether it has been the crusade approach of Billy Graham or the more process-orientated courses such as Alpha, the task of winning people to faith has received huge attention. It is very understandable that this should be so but there has been correspondingly less attention paid to the process of discipleship making.

It is certainly true that some parachurch agencies, notably the Navigators and YWAM, have given high priority to this task, but to some extent that has stood in contrast with the practice of the local church. As I have talked with the leaders of local churches in a number of Western nations, few if any, have been able to point me to any substantial or significant discipleship processes in the churches that they know. In much the same way, leaders from nations that are experiencing significant evangelistic growth, for example, in Africa and South America, report a similar difficulty with the task of discipleship training.

It is perhaps not too surprising that churches in lands that have inherited Western approaches to the faith might be experiencing some of the same problems as the Western church. Given that Jesus called people to be disciples and not just believers, and given that the early church gave high priority to the preparation of the new believers or catechumens, what has caused this present difficulty?

There would seem to be two very different kinds of problem. The first is the historic difficulty that flowed from past successes. The very fact that the church was able to influence culture strongly in past centuries, meant that to some extent, at least in the past, it was possible to rely on the culture to disciple new converts. The soaking of the minds and hearts of individuals in a broader culture that was formed partly by Christian imagination meant that instruction in the faith became much more like church membership classes than discipleship training. That was perhaps naïve but certainly understandable.

The pattern in the recent past in the West has been that of the preparation of young teenagers for confirmation in churches with paedo-baptist traditions, and baptism by immersion in baptistic churches. A substantial tradition of adult confirmations and baptisms is more common now but it was not always so and discipleship processes are still influenced by the tradition of preparation for Christian initiation surrounding young teenagers.

The second and more recent problem relates to the growing distance between Christianity and Western culture. We have now reached the point where becoming a disciple of Jesus Christ is more clearly counter-cultural than it has been for many years. In the now well-known phrase of Hauerwas, we are called to be 'resident aliens'.[1]

Culture wars

Thinking through the business of helping new converts to be counter-cultural is almost an unknown discipline and requires some fresh thinking. If we are to be successful in this exercise, then at the very least we need to have some awareness of the tendencies in our culture that act corrosively against Christian discipleship. In the very broadest sense there is a clash of narratives between a secular and a Christian vision of the world.

A secular view of life seeks to de-sacralize the world and amounts to a campaign to marginalize religion of all kinds. In the words of one observer of a secular perspective, it offers a very limited space to a religious perspective. 'Religion can survive, but only in forms that are secularized, sectarian or fundamentalist.'[2] A secular perspective offers a very different answer than Christianity to ultimate questions. These questions can be summarized as: who are we (identity), where are we going (destiny), what are we here for (purpose) and how do we live together (community)?

That alternative secular, and currently dominant narrative contains a number of key themes that emerge as it seeks to answer these ultimate questions. It is not possible in a book such as this to engage in a comprehensive analysis of Western secular thought but four themes are worth mentioning.

Radical individualism

The thrust of modernity has driven a view of life that emphasizes the autonomous individual. Just as science seeks to dissect and understand life on the basis of the smallest unit, so society is also understood in terms of its component parts rather than from the perspective of its wholeness. It is almost as though we can only be truly human if we are disconnected from others, entirely autonomous, completely self-sufficient and alone.

Some time ago, the present Pope (Benedict) engaged in an analysis of the novel *Steppenwolf* by Herman Hesse. Essentially his argument is as follows. Steppenwolf is the ultimate autonomous individual. In that sense it is a novel that encapsulates the spirit of our age. However, aloneness eventually becomes loneliness. In time, loneliness becomes isolation and despair. That isolation and despair leads to a sense of boredom, a boredom so acute that only death itself offers any sense of thrill or excitement.

It is this radical individualism that therefore produces what some have called a 'culture of death', an obsession with the ultimate thrill of death on the one hand and a boredom that devalues life on the other. So whether it is high risk behaviour or an easy acceptance of euthanasia or abortion, ultimately the autonomous individual embraces death rather than life.

The Christian narrative always stresses the importance of community. For Christians, the individual can only be completely fulfilled in relationship with others. The idea of radical individuality makes incomplete sense in the Christian tradition. Although it is certainly true that each individual is valuable and therefore life is honoured, that value needs to be seen in relation to the whole of society. For the Christian there is always such a thing as society.

The consumer heart
Many have observed that the Western world has shifted from being a culture that has production at its heart to one that sees the individual as a consumer. Indeed, in a post-industrial age where the production of goods is moving increasingly to poorer eastern nations, the West has moved to being a provider of services, whether financial, intellectual or located in entertainment of various sorts. We are now an information society much more than an industrial society.

The shift in perspective from production to consumption has a huge impact on the way we see the world. Our desires and wants become much more important than our contribution. It has led to what some have called the elimination of delayed gratification. Recently I drove past a store in the United States which proudly proclaimed, 'We sell more of everything.' The idea that we can have more and more and that we do not have to wait, assisted by the credit card which 'takes the waiting out of wanting', is pervasive and potentially destructive.

Child psychologists point to the learning of the principle of delayed gratification as an important stage in child development. It is an important lesson. The toddler begins to learn that if they are given ten sweets (candies) they might be better not to eat them all at once. They can save some to enjoy later. They might even want to save some until after their next meal. It can become a reward to be enjoyed later. That realization represents a significant shift in perception.

The failure to learn that lesson or to have it undermined by a ruthlessly pervasive consumer story, which discourages delayed gratification, leads in time to the creation of a generation of adults who in some respects have not learnt how to grow up. Too many adults in the West are out of control in terms of spending, eating and sensory desire.

In some very important respects, the consumer society becomes the addictive society. The addictions are multiple and not always obvious. They can be easy to recognize addictions to alcohol, drugs and food but they can just as easily encompass an addiction to work or even to thrill-seeking. The adrenalin rush feels just as wonderful for the adrenalin junky as the release of endorphins for the addicted long-distance runner. Curiously, that which was supposed to lead to our happiness actually leads to despair, brokenness and the need for therapy of various kinds. The addictive society produces the recovery group society.

By contrast, the Christian story emphasizes self-denial, fasting, discipline, a rhythm in life and a routine to prayer. While these disciplines are focused on what they achieve in us, the intention is partly a change in us for the sake of others. It is all too easy to see how the Christian message can be seduced by the consumer story. Christianity itself can be just one more rush of adrenalin – this time a spiritual rush that seeks more and more spiritual mountain-top experiences before burning out with spiritual exhaustion. The Jesus is good for you, or things go better with Jesus Christ message is profoundly true at one level but packaged as a consumer artefact, it is destructively untrue. Nor can Christianity packaged as a consumer message compete at that level. There will always be a more seductive package awaiting the consumer than a faith that makes some demands on the consumer's time, concentration and allegiance.

A world of rights
The notion that human beings can enjoy a set of inalienable human rights designed to safeguard life and lead to happiness, represents a story of a commitment to human dignity and liberty. Its most comprehensive expression in terms of a whole society, a framework of law and government and as a democratic ideal, has been seen in the shaping of the modern United States of America. It is substantially that ideal that has been exported around the world as a Western way of life.

At its best, the emphasis on human rights is commendable and entirely consistent with a Christian view of the dignity and worth of all people. However, at its worst, in an unhealthy alliance with individualism and consumerism the idea of the rights of an individual person quickly deteriorates to a new level of selfishness that seeks to use the law as a weapon to be wielded by the powerful. Under such a regime, 'my rights' becomes simply an extension of what I think I want or even believe I deserve.

The reason for this unhealthy departure from a noble tradition is that the championing of human rights depended on an older tradition that stressed the importance of corporate and personal responsibility.[3] Those who formed the notion of modern human rights assumed that the older tradition of mutual care and duty would remain in place. They certainly never intended rights to replace responsibilities but only to balance them.

Unfortunately that is what has sometimes taken place with terrible consequences for a continued sense of compassion and care for the stranger. What some have called 'the community of strangers' requires an inherited community and cannot be understood without reference to previous generations. The undermining of an older Christian tradition of care for others has twisted the concern for human rights such that it has become an argument for self-care.[4]

An unfettered stress on rights without a nurturing sense of community stresses 'my rights' and undermines the rights of others. In such a situation it is the poor, the distressed, the refugee, the prisoner, the homeless and the hungry who lose out. It is precisely these groups – the strangers – that the Christian gospel seeks to enfranchise. The despised and rejected hold a special place of honour in the Christian tradition. It is our treatment of these outcast groups that becomes the measure for a Christian understanding of society.

Discipleship is therefore partly about developing a healthy sense of responsibility in relation to the rights of others and not first and foremost about the promotion of our own rights. That way of thinking is, for the moment, somewhat antithetical in relation to our culture. However, we should not be too entirely discouraged. As the response to the 'Make Poverty History' ('One' in the USA) campaign has demonstrated, a sense of altruistic idealism can still be activated in the West.

Suspicion of tradition

The ability to draw on older traditions of wisdom concerning the duties of citizens is further undermined by a profound suspicion of tradition and authority. The Enlightenment project has always contained a significant orientation toward the future and a corresponding attempt to escape the past. A love affair with that which is new suggests that the future will always contain that which is better and by contrast the past has little of worth to offer. The future is associated with progress, liberty, prosperity and a kind of utopianism that has proved to be astonishingly enduring in the face of actual evidence that suggests a contrary experience.

Only in the twentieth century has there come a growing sense of foreboding about what the future could hold – a distopia – without a corresponding embrace of wisdom from the past. The past is sometimes romanticized but not really taken seriously. It becomes a pastiche rather than a profound understanding of tradition. In common parlance the word tradition is associated with all that is dull and lacking in inspiration. It is acceptable for royal weddings and state occasions but not really as an active ingredient in everyday life.

In part, the United States was founded as an attempt to escape 'old' Europe and Europeans were encouraged to embrace the new world order that America was shaping, partly in competition with European states. Christianity in nineteenth-century America was also significantly shaped by a concern for the future – often a millenarian future. Fascination with the second coming underpinned much popular thinking about matters of faith. Christians were moved to shape society in preparation for the return of Christ. Christian views of paradise were just as powerful as secular views of utopia.

The Christian vision of a just society was something that captured the aspiration of many, both in Europe and in America, until the First World War. Since that time, a growing disenchantment with Christianity has tended to place Christianity alongside the other traditions that the modern and now postmodern world are trying to escape. Postmodernity has tended to add a suspicion of authority as a powerful theme to accompany the existing suspicion that modernity had engendered in relation to tradition. These two themes, tradition and authority, are increasingly seen as two sides of the same thing. As we will explore in a moment, discipleship processes critically depend on an appreciation of the wisdom that comes from a community of faith. There is an inbuilt prejudice in our culture that militates against drawing on the riches of tradition.

Habits of the heart

Given that there are some deeply ingrained features in Western culture that make it more difficult to produce disciples as compared with religious consumers, how can we begin to think more constructively and creatively about the task? Traditionally there has been a tendency to think in terms of correct belief leading to correct behaviour. In other words, sound doctrine leads to right thought which leads to forms of behaving which look Christian. That has sometimes been formulated as Believe, Behave, Belong. Most Christian churches have tended to want people to believe the right things so that they will live in an appropriate way and therefore they will become suitable people to admit as members. More recently the work of Grace Davies and others has suggested that belonging to the community is more important as a factor in forming behaviour and that correct belief tends to flow from changed behaviour. The pattern has therefore been reformulated as Belong, Behave, Believe.[5]

Lest this should become a rather sterile debate about which formula works best, it is important to note an older tradition that emphasizes the complexity of the relationship between the community of faith, spiritual practices, structures of belief, different ways of learning and the importance of a personal relationship with a teacher or spiritual mentor. In other words, thought has been given to the way in which Jesus formed disciples. The process that he used was not one-dimensional but had a degree of organic complexity in terms of the journey that he took his disciples on.

Sometimes Jesus taught his followers with parables, and on other occasions by example. It is clear that the disciples did not just listen but they also attempted to put the teachings of Jesus into practice. That attempt to hear and do led to many practical questions that were teased out in conversation with Jesus. Becoming a disciple does not happen in a six-week, ten-week or thirteen-week course, helpful as these resources might be along the way.

The complexity of this process needs to be understood in relation to our earlier discussion about the assumption of an older tradition that underpins modern ideas such as human rights. The sociologist Robert Bellah has considered the relationship of an older Christian discourse to present-day attempts to reconcile individualism with a broader commitment to society in present-day America.[6]

His proposition is that it is impossible to create responsible citizens without creating the 'habits of the heart' that were taken for granted at the time of the foundation of the American constitution. For Bellah and his circle of contributors, no amount of appeal to patriotism, duty, enlightened self-interest or even idealism has any impact on creating the kind of good citizens that are needed if society is to function healthily. In other words, we cannot guarantee our future as individuals unless we know how to live in community.

The work of Bellah has been mirrored to some extent by the work of Robert Putnam in his book *Bowling Alone*.[7] The title of the book stems from an observation that whereas in the 1950s nearly everyone who visited bowling alleys in the United States played in teams, from the 1990s onwards, the majority of customers were playing entirely alone.

Putnam is arguing the case for the construction of social capital. His contention is that society needs all kinds of capital – financial, political, industrial, physical in the sense of roads and transportation systems, intellectual and many others, and that the place of social capital has been overlooked. He makes the case that society cannot function without social capital. He defines the term as the willingness of individuals to help others, to be involved, to volunteer and to serve others. For Putnam, social capital was overlooked and unseen when it was available in abundance but its gradual shrinkage is causing society to become unglued.

Because there is a strong connectivity between the abandoned 'habits of the heart' described by Bellah and the attitudes that lead to the formation of social capital and the same assumptions that shape disciples, it is potentially very helpful to understand what these habits and attitudes are. This is precisely where we start to run into some difficulty. Not all who are interested in 'habits of the heart' agree precisely about their formulation and content.

Complete agreement is not necessary for us to gain some feel for the habits and attitudes that are sought after. Clifton Taulbert attempts to develop Bellah's work and apply it to the building of strong families and communities. Taulbert lists eight habits as follows:

- A nurturing attitude: unselfish caring, supportiveness and a willingness to share time
- Dependability: being there for others
- Responsibility: demonstrating a personal commitment to each task
- Friendship: taking pleasure in the company of others and sharing their experiences both good and bad
- Brotherhood: extending a welcome to those who may be different from yourself

- High expectations: believing that others can be successful and encouraging them
- Courage: speaking out on behalf of others
- Hope: believing in tomorrow.[8]

Others have taken a similar approach and attempted to apply some of these attributes to particular situations. For example, there has been a good amount of work thinking through the application of habits of the heart to school situations. Costanoa High School in Santa Cruz, California, have distilled these thoughts in terms of four major areas:

- Integrity
- Communication
- Being a good neighbour
- Creating a safe environment.[9]

At first sight these two lists look very different from one another. However, the commonality revolves around how we act toward and think of others such that supportive community is created. With all of that in mind, what might it look like to apply 'habits of heart' thinking to the discipleship area? What fundamental habits do we need to inculcate in terms of actions, attitudes and beliefs? If we can inculcate good habits in these three areas it is likely to have a significant impact on personal lifestyle and the creation of Christian community.

Habits of the disciple

As we think about the kind of habits of the heart that we want to inculcate, we might want to think about the kind of Christians we would like to have as our friends and indeed that we might like to become over time. Perhaps we can sum that up no better than pointing to the fruit of the Spirit: love, joy, peace, patience, kindness, goodness, faithfulness, gentleness, self-control. These are all positive qualities. There are, of course, also practices that we should stop as well as qualities we should develop. The ten commandments deal very solidly with wrong actions that must stop.

If the fruit of the Spirit were to be present in our lives and in the lives of those around us we could be confident of building a mature community of disciples, possibly disciples with the capacity to change the world. Before considering how we might go about that, let's take some time to look at the ideal. There are three core issues that need to be addressed.

1. Personal foundational disciplines
There are certain foundational disciplines that need to be routinely exercised if we are to be successful in any area of life. The following is not an exhaustive list of these disciplines but they are an indication of basic skills that need to be learnt and practised. In times past most of these could be assumed but it seems that they no longer can be.

Management of time
Time is one of the most precious commodities that we have in our lives. It is a resource that is entirely finite. Self-discipline in our use of time makes a huge difference to our ability to make progress in life. Most of us are aware of our tendency to waste time. We might also note the areas where we procrastinate, avoiding doing the things that we don't like to do.

Management of money
Finances represent another precious resource that we need to use well. Paying attention to financial disciplines enables us to be free of the terrible worry and oppression that can come when our finances are out of control. For the Christian disciple, all of our possessions belong to God and our responsibility is to use the money that God has given to

us as wise stewards. A wise use of money allows us to tithe. In fact we could almost say that the practice of tithing is given to us as a mechanism for ensuring that our finances are in order since few people can tithe easily without their finances being well thought through.

Rhythm of life
We all need a good rhythm in our lives, a balance between work and play. We need to make room for recreation as well as for work of various kinds. For the Christian a healthy rhythm includes a place for regular worship and prayer. Examining the overall balance of our life and making the necessary adjustments keeps us healthy. We might ask ourselves whether there are any addictions in our life that act to throw our life out of balance. That includes an addiction to the workplace where our employer may have a tendency to ask of us more than they are entitled to.

Hard work
Strangely, hard work is good for us and is not something to be avoided. That does not mean we should become workaholics. Paying attention to balance in our life should avoid overwork but few people who achieve much in life do so without significant effort.

Persistence
Periods of hard work do not by themselves guarantee success. Our hard work can be misdirected and we certainly need to be open to review our activity, but within that we do need to learn persistence. Initial failure should not lead to us giving up in despair.

2. Relationships with others
If we are able to put the basic disciplines outlined above into practice that helps us to imagine how we might relate to others. What would others appreciate as basic

behaviours in us? What do we expect to see in others? As I think of those that I look to for inspiration and guidance, I would say that they consistently demonstrate the following qualities in their relationships with others:

- They tell the truth with sensitivity
- They do what they say they will do if they possibly can
- They speak well of others
- They listen attentively to what others have to say
- They encourage others and work for their success.

3. *The practice of goodness*
Developing the qualities listed above helps us in the practice of goodness. Hopefully we can help to develop people such that kindness flows naturally. It should be our first instinct to help others. Naturally, help needs to be offered wisely but few people have been ruined by kindness, love and affection.

Developing the processes

If these are some of the attributes, skills and disciplines that we are hoping to see in the coming generations of disciples of Christ, what are some of the processes that need to be employed to bring this about? Three areas are important.

1. *Accountability structures*
There is very little lasting change likely to take place in the lives of most people without there being some accountability in the process. As I look back on my own life, I can see how my family life, experiences of marriage, education and work have helped me to be accountable in some key areas of life. There have been few accountability structures in place in the area of faith. Fortunately for me, I have enjoyed some strong friendships with Christian brothers

who have challenged me graciously but firmly when they have seen me needing to make changes in my life. While I am grateful to these friends it would have been helpful to have had some accountability structures in place in my early Christian life.

What do accountability structures accomplish and what do they look like? To be effective, an accountability group is going to be small, possibly no more than three or four people. They need to contain a facilitator who is more mature than new Christians in the group and they almost certainly need to be single-gender groups. They also need to meet regularly and frequently. Accountability works best when the individuals in the group make their own decisions about the changes they want to see and therefore construct the agenda that they want to be held accountable for. There is no need to be too ambitious in goal-setting. Consistent small changes over time that are achievable are preferable to huge leaps of faith that are unlikely to be achieved.

For example, developing a rhythm of prayer is essential. A basic rhythm might be to set aside some time every day, a longer period once a week and an even longer time once a month. Ten minutes a day would be an achievable beginning. Half an hour once a week would be a new experience for many, and finding half a day once a month, a significant leap for most. Of course, if that remains the pattern for twenty years then one might judge that not much progress has been made, but exponential progress is often more effective than sudden change. Of course, if a new convert is suddenly and joyously engaging in longer periods of daily prayer, no one should discourage them but usually that is not the case.

We can use accountability groups to begin to explore areas of self-denial. These could include times of fasting but they might also include the gradual facing of many areas of addiction that need to become subject to self-discipline.

2. Small group structures

Having said that accountability structures need to be very small in size, there is a role in the discipleship process for small groups that could be as many as twelve to fifteen in number. These groups do not need to be single gender in make-up. Small groups can be used to make progress in four key areas:

Knowing the Scripture

Exposure to the great stories of the Bible informs our Christian imagination and provides potential disciples with a huge reservoir from which to draw lessons for life. As N. T. Wright puts it, 'We read scripture in order to be refreshed in our memory and understanding of the story within which we ourselves are actors, to be reminded where it has come from, where it is going to, and hence what our own part within it ought to be.'[10]

Listening to God

The discipline of learning how to hear God speaking is much easier to explore and experiment with in a small group than in a public worship setting. Helping people to hear God such that they begin to see the world from a spiritual dimension acts as a powerful counterbalance to a culture which gives scant regard to the idea of a divine perspective on life. Awaking people to a sense of God's presence such that there can be a regular referencing to God during the course of an ordinary day helps followers of Jesus to do just that – to follow his voice and guidance.

Resolving conflict

No matter how effective our discipleship processes there will always be some conflict in the body of Christ. One could even argue that conflict is God's tool for rubbing off our sharp edges so that we are able to develop the fruit of the Spirit. In fact, when one looks at the fruit of the Spirit, it is difficult to see how we could develop any of those fruits without it taking place in the context of a relationship with others. Conflict needs to be seen as an opportunity for deepening understanding, not as an occasion to leave the church.

Gift identification
We are called to give service to others but the best service we can give will stem from the gifts we have been given by God. Helping disciples to discover their gift areas assists the process of locating them in areas of service and mission.

3. Spiritual direction
The intention of good discipleship processes is both to draw out and develop the fruit of the Spirit but also to help a disciple to know themselves. There are many ways of helping people to be realistic about who they are, and honest about their failings. We have listed some of these approaches above. The discipline of spiritual direction is a relatively new experience for many Christians though it has been present in Catholic circles for many years. Perhaps the best known sources are Benedictine and Ignatian models of spiritual direction. The intention of spiritual direction is to deepen and mature the growing sense of listening to God that will have been developing in the life of disciples in the preceding processes. Spiritual direction helps to give a wellspring of refreshment for the long road ahead.

Resources

Traditionally there have been very few resources available to help us in the disciple-making task. The Alpha course is helpful in setting the expectation for what a discipleship course might look like – the setting in small groups, the expectation that discussion will take place and some encounter with the Holy Spirit is all helpful in laying the groundwork for a discipleship experience. Two resources that are very different and will perhaps work for different types of churches are:

- The Emmaus Course published by Church House Publishing in the UK. This is a two-year course and is based around a leader's guidebook and participants' handbooks.
- The Freedom in Christ Discipleship Course, written by Neil Anderson and Steve Goss and published by Monarch Books. This is a thirteen-week starter course which contains DVDs, a leader's guide with a presentation CD-ROM, and a participants' workbook.

It is possible that by the time you have read this chapter on discipleship that you will feel less like planting a church. I hope that is not your reaction and it is certainly not my intention. However, if we want to plant healthy churches that contain the possibility of reproduction then we do need to figure out how the discipleship processes are going to be put in place. It is one element in the total picture as we estimate and gather the resources that we are going to need for the journey.

Notes
1. Hauerwas, Stanley, W and Willimon, William H, *Resident Aliens: Life in the Christian Colony*, Abingdon Press, 1989
2. McLeod, Hugh and Ustorf Werner (Eds), *The Decline of Christendom in Western Europe 1750–2000*, Cambridge University Press, 2003, p. 205
3. Guiness, Os explores this theme in more detail in, *The American Hour: A Time of Reckoning and the Once and Future Role of Faith*, Simon and Schuster, 1992
4. For a more detailed discussion of these issues see Roger Scruton, *The West and the Rest: Globalization and the Terrorist Threat*, ISI Books, 2002,

particularly a chapter on Enlightenment, Citizenship and Loyalty, pp. 41 ff.
5. Davie, Grace, *Religion in Britain Since 1945: Believing Without Belonging*, Blackwell, 1994
6. Bellah, Robert, N et al, *Habits of the Heart*, Berkeley: University of California Press, 1985.
7. Putnam, Robert, *Bowling Alone: The Collapse and Revival of American Community*, Simon and Schuster, 2000.
8. Taulbert, Clifton, see an article in which he explores themes themes on, www.family.org/fofmag/sh/a0023960.cfm
9. Costanoa High School in Santa Cruz, California, see www.costanoa.santacruz.k12.ca.us/habits
10. N. T. Wright, Scripture and the Authority of God, SPCK, 2005, p. 84f.

Chapter Seven
The Spiritual Life

I have just finished examining six major books on church planting, all of them very good books. Not one of these books had a chapter on anything that resembled prayer and the spiritual life. It is not that prayer is never mentioned, but more often than not it is assumed. It strikes me that there are two very different problems for the church planter in relation to the spiritual life.

First, I sometimes see prayer and the spiritual life treated in a mechanistic manner. In other words, if we want certain results we must complete our action checklist and prayer is on there somewhere. Do these things and you will get the right results. Anyone who has been a church planter will soon realize that a mechanistic approach to the planting process – especially in the area of prayer – is likely to lead to severe disappointment and possibly to acute depression.

Second, it is possible that an assumption is made that the church planter, because he or she is a mature Christian already, has a well-established spiritual life. That is not a safe assumption. Dr Patrick Keifert of Church Innovations, has conducted a significant survey of the spiritual practices of church leaders and discovered that in the overwhelming majority of cases clergy had very little long-term spiritual disciplines in place.[1] Prayer and the other disciplines were entered into occasionally and superficially. Although there is no separate data for church planters, even if we were to assume a much higher spiritual maturity among church planters, it is unlikely that the results will be much different.

There are a number of very common reasons why this is the case. First, the spiritual life is not easy and rarely comes naturally to adults. Second, teaching on spirituality is often absent or poor. Third, the pressures and busyness of life and ministry cause us, unwisely, not to invest time in this area. Even as you read this chapter you might well be tempted to think to yourself, this is the chapter I will skip or possibly come back to later. There is so much else to implement I can only absorb so much at a time.

In reality a church planter needs to give more attention to the spiritual life than to any other area. There are at least four good reasons why this is so. First, the challenges in terms of spiritual warfare are much more acute when we are attempting something that is groundbreaking – taking new territory. The kingdom of God is not expanded without conflict in the spiritual realm.[2] Second, the structures of church life are largely absent in the early days of the church plant and therefore the planter needs to construct some personal spiritual structures to act as a resource. Third, planting a church is very hard work. It can be enjoyable and it should be but it will usually take most people to the edge of their personal resources. The resource of the spiritual life is essential if we are not to be damaged by running on empty. Fourth, much of the success that will come in the planting process will flow more from who we are as people than on what we do as planters. People will see our character long before they see the programme of the developing church. The spiritual life shapes who we are and through that lens, shapes what we do.

What do we mean by the spiritual life?

There is a tendency to think about the spiritual life entirely on the basis of the things that we do such as prayer, fasting, meditation and worship. While these are helpful mechanisms about which we shall say more later, they are not themselves the core of the spiritual life. In an important sense, everyone has a spirituality simply because our spirituality is the total way in which we relate and respond to life out of who we are as people.

Our spirituality can be described as the way in which we see the world, others, God and even ourselves. That way of seeing is shaped by our values, attitudes and our viewpoint in terms of meaning. What we think, believe and feel about our world has a profound impact on the way in which we relate to others, to the material world and to God. These deeply held commitments impact our decisions about our careers, our ambitions and our priorities.

What is at issue is not whether we have a spirituality – because we all have one – but rather how we can understand and develop that spirituality and subsequently how we can help our spirituality to be as healthy as possible. Our spirituality is reflected in the relationship between who we are and what we do. The things that we do flow out of who we are but also continue to shape and reinforce who we are.

A healthy Christian spirituality is centred in our relationship with God. If that centre of love for God is not present we have a significant difficulty. A healthy spirituality cannot be centred in fear of God, or flow out of a sense of duty alone. Our priority is to be devoted to God rather than to good deeds, or to the institution that we serve, or even to other people.

There is nothing wrong with serving the church, acting charitably and serving others but these things need to flow from and be shaped by the priority of our love for God. At its heart, Christian spirituality is concerned with the inward journey. The intention of the inward journey is not a preoccupation with self but rather a reorientation of the self such that we can then journey outwards in a positive and healthy way. We need to know ourselves in order to know others and we need to be able to love ourselves in order to love others.

The process of coming to know ourselves is what the spiritual disciplines are intended to accomplish. They are not ends in themselves but rather they assist us towards the end of loving God more completely and allowing the experience of that love to shape and inform our understanding of ourselves and our world.

Forces of destruction

One of the foremost contemporary writers on spirituality, Richard Foster, provocatively named one his books on spirituality *Money, Sex and Power*. Here is why he did so:

> The crying need today is for people of faith to live faithfully. This is true in all spheres of human existence, but is particularly true with regards to money, sex and power. No issues touch us more profoundly or more universally. No themes are more inseparably intertwined. No topics cause more controversy. No human realities have greater power to bless or to curse. No three things have been more sought after or are more in need of a Christian response.[3]

Richard Foster goes on to explain how these areas of existence are closely connected, indeed interwoven with one another. He illustrates how these themes emerge in classical literature that deals with the human condition. In particular he points out that the writer Dostoevsky deals with these ethical themes in his masterpiece *The Idiot*. But why should these issues concern us, what have they to do with spirituality and why should church planters pay attention to them?

In the previous chapter we looked at the tendencies in our culture to combine radical individualism, with conspicuous consumption both within the context of an emphasis on our rights and a suspicion of tradition. It doesn't take much imagination to see how these themes tend towards an abuse of money, sex and power. It becomes our right to indulge our fantasies in the pursuit of our right of happiness. Traditional restraints are seen as old-fashioned and unduly restrictive and it takes little effort to throw them off. Unfortunately the deep well of unhappiness in our culture is often related to an inability to use the gifts of money, sex and power well. That which was given for our good – to serve us – too often becomes the master.

Christian leaders are in the difficult position of needing to bring a healing balm to a culture injured by excess and yet are subject to exactly the same pressures because we also live in the culture that we seek to minister to. A well-known Christian leader told me recently of how he contacted the large group of fellow leaders who graduated from Bible college with him some thirty-five years ago only to discover that he was the only one still active in ministry. What had happened to the others? In nearly every case, their inability to deal well with money, sex and power had led to the destruction of their ministry and in some cases to a loss of faith.

A healthy spirituality is required both as an antidote to excess but also as a means of generating balance such that these potentially good gifts can be used wisely and well. In one sense every Christian leader needs to pay attention to these issues but the church planter has an additional set of challenges. Leaders in existing churches at least have a system of safeguards and accountabilities in place that can help them to tackle difficult issues. They may choose to disregard these safeguards and we have to be realistic and admit that no matter what structures are put in place the devious can always circumvent them. In one sense we are only as accountable as we really wish to be.

But many church planters don't have any day-to-day frameworks in place to hold them accountable. That is problematic for two reasons. First, not to have a safety net while we are planting lays us open to what we might call the wiles of the evil one. It is essential to construct significant layers of accountability. Second, as we establish the church, we tend to reflect our own discipline, or lack of it, in the structures we develop as the church is planted. The planter who has not paid attention to their personal accountability in the light of spiritual challenges is unlikely to lay a healthy foundation for the future. You owe it to yourself and to future generations to equip yourself to deal with the spiritual challenges of the role and the task. Money, sex and power will be your point of vulnerability without that strong accountability in place.

Resources for the spiritual life

The intention of the spiritual life is not to become disconnected with the real world but rather to live a full human life in relationship with God. The mature Christian has come to understand that we cannot be fully human without a divine perspective. The goal towards which we strive is the imitation of Christ – Christ-likeness in our attitudes, behaviour and character.

The fundamental concerns of all human beings in relation to our desires, identity, destiny and purpose for living are all illuminated and given greater depth as we seek to imitate Christ. The key questions that flow from these areas, what do I want?, who am I?, where am I heading?, and why am I here? are all better informed as we come to see that God has a plan and a purpose for our lives. We discover the answers to these lifelong questions as we learn to become centred in God rather than in ourselves, or worse still, in our fears, worries and anxieties about life.

The basic precondition for becoming centred in God

lies in our ability to understand the value of solitude as compared with loneliness. Solitude involves learning how to be alone with God. That is not something we learn from the secular world and yet it is a basic prerequisite for living a healthy spiritual life. It is in the silent place that we learn about ourselves in relation to God. The experience of being alone (as compared with lonely) can be frightening for some, for many it is a completely new experience to spend significant amounts of time, several hours or days, alone with God. The context that works best for us will vary according to our personality. Some prefer the isolation of the monastery cell or chapel, others do better being alone in the countryside or on the beach.

Where we are does not matter but the experience of being alone with God is important for our spiritual growth. As we spend time alone we may find that we begin to be aware of anger or frustration. These negative emotions are not to be avoided, they represent the personal monsters that are present in all of us. If they are not confronted and understood in a healthy way then they lie hidden and can ambush us when we are unaware of their presence. It is these negative emotions that lie hidden that can distort our use of money, sex and power. Once we understand better the source or reasons for our anger, fears, frustrations and desires then we can learn how to offer them to God.

Solitude draws us to silence. It is surprising how many people, when facing being alone in the context of their own home, will avoid silence by turning on a radio or the television. It is not that they want to watch a programme or listen to a particular piece of music, it is just that silence is difficult for many. Even if we don't actually create some sound, we can turn to the sounds of other voices in a book or a newspaper. These are all ways of avoiding the experience of spending time with God. Solitude – time with God – requires an absence of the normal sounds of life that crash in and distract our attention from God.

As we seek both solitude and silence – creative times alone with God, we can begin to employ a range of disciplines that help us to make the most of this time. A descriptive list of such disciplines follows[4]. As you look at the list, remember that it is not important to use all twenty-two disciplines in equal measure. You may do so over the whole period of your life, but rather it is more helpful to choose from the list a few disciplines that you will find particularly helpful at this stage in your journey. Don't get stuck in a rut. Return to the list from time to time and test whether it is opportune to experiment with some additional or different disciplines from the list, especially those that you are not so familiar with.

1. Setting the agenda

In order to help you take your spiritual disciplines seriously, it is important to have a keen sense of what the issues are. Perhaps your first venture into the spiritual life could be to prayerfully ask God to help you identify the issues in your life that you think you need to work on with God's help. Write these down as a list that you can review from time to time.

2. Review the diary

An intention to devote time to the spiritual life needs to be accompanied by action. You almost certainly will need to make space in your diary if your intended pattern of prayer and time alone with God is going to take place. You might want to be radical and rearrange your existing appointments otherwise you do need to put time into the diary so that it does not continue to be full to the point of being crammed with activity.

3. Private prayer

Perhaps your times of private prayer have become somewhat dry. This might be a good opportunity to begin again in a fresh way. This might be the time to pray in unfamiliar ways. You could try using a set daily office or even writing some of your prayers down. You could try prayer walking or create a sacred space in your own home. Some find it helpful to create a *postinia* (a Russian word for cell or chapel) – you could adopt your garden shed!

4. Worship and liturgy
All worship has its own liturgy. Even if the liturgy is not written down with set words, there normally will be a pattern that is familiar to those who attend your church. This might be a time to experience worship from a tradition that is radically different than your own. Perhaps there is a time in the week or even on a Sunday where traditions that are different from yours have a worship service that you could attend. A few years ago I was surprised to find the Episcopal Cathedral in Seattle packed on a Sunday night for a traditional service of compline. Even more surprising was that most of the worshippers were in their teens or early twenties and many had been brought up in more contemporary evangelical settings – what some like to call 'happy clappy Christianity'.

5. Reflective reading
Using a book that contains meditations can also be helpful to orientate our hearts and minds to issues that we might not otherwise consider. Some use the classic writings from the desert fathers or even from some of the medieval mystics. Favourites from more recent times include Thomas Merton, Henri Nouwen and Dietrich Bonhoeffer. These short daily readings offer spiritual wisdom and food to refresh the soul.

6. The contemplative life
Meditation and contemplation are two aspects of prayer that are slightly different and can usefully be used in relation to each other. The basic idea of meditation

is to take an idea, either from our own life experience, or from a passage of Scripture or one of the spiritual readings that we have been using and think about that one idea – meditate on it – allow yourself to see how God might want to apply that truth in your life, or even see an aspect of that truth that you have not seen before. The issue is giving yourself enough time to chew the issue through.

Contemplation is closer to emptying yourself of your own thoughts to allow God to speak to you. The discipline involves placing yourself before God and allowing him to speak. For those who are not accustomed to the process of contemplation, it can follow more naturally a period of meditation.

7. The use of Scripture

As we have indicated, Holy Scripture can be used in meditation but there are other ways to engage with the Bible. We need to ensure that our spiritual life is fed by Scripture. These are the reminders of the activity of God, the stories of his interaction with his people that feed our spiritual imagination. The regular reading of Scripture such that we allow it to speak to our situation, to our lives is vital. The Psalms were a particular joy to the Celtic saints. They used them more than any other part of the Bible.

8. The call to work

Our work should be a means of communing with God. We can view our work as something of a drudgery, and possibly the coming of the industrial revolution with its accompanying dehumanization of workers on the production track helped to downgrade the value of work in the eyes of many. But work does not have to be merely an ordeal to be endured simply as a means to obtain a pay packet. Viewed sacramentally our work can be a means of giving glory to God. We ought to be able to thank God for the opportunity to work and to therefore work in such a way that we use our work as an offering of thanks.

9. Confession
The practice of confession in terms of confessing sin to another human being has largely been lost to the Protestant community as a result of the changes at the time of the Reformation. But that should not mean that Protestants do not confess sin to God. It is possible that as believers we do not confess on a regular basis as much as we should do. The prayer of the desert fathers, 'Kyrie eleison – Lord have mercy', suggests that mercy is necessary because we have sinned and fallen short of the glory of God. It is healthy to remind ourselves of our shortcomings, the areas where we need both mercy and succour to help us in our walk with God. You might want to ask yourself where regular confession fits in your spiritual life. Would it be advantageous to include confession in your weekly devotions, possibly as a prelude to receiving Holy Communion?

10. Penance
The idea of penance has been devalued because of its association with punishment. Some of the Celtic suggestions for penance in relation to the Celtic monastic orders seem very harsh to our ears but that should not cause us to forget the value of these exercises. Penance is not so much a punishment as an attempt to address addictions and bad habits. The point about various addictions is that we tend to lean on destructive behaviours rather than leaning on God. The voluntary renunciation of certain habits and behaviours, if even just for a season, helps us to recover our sense of reliance on God alone.

11. Dealing with pride
One of the great dangers for strong and able leaders lies precisely in the fact that their obvious strength of leadership will be widely admired. That can easily lead to an unjustified pride. The advice of Scripture to count others as better than yourself is wisdom indeed. Another way of putting it

is to say, 'Never believe your own propaganda!' Actively consider those you know whose achievements are more modest than your own and think about what you might admire in them.

One of the people that I most value having met is a person who most people in the world would have written off as having lived a life that was without significance. She died around the turn of the century and the church was packed for her funeral. We all loved her, not for her fame and achievements but for her commitment to prayer, simplicity and love for everyone. She suffered huge amounts of illness but never complained. There are many respects in which I would like to be more like her. The regular practice of humility stops us seeing ourselves as saviours of the world. It is always wise to remember that saviours often end up being crucified!

12. Self denial

The very physicality of fasting means that it is a useful discipline for believers. Some sources suggest that many in the early church fasted three days a week – Mondays, Wednesdays and Fridays. In time, Friday became the customary fast day in the church, associated as it was with the death of Jesus. As more time passed, a complete daily fast from sunrise to sunset became an abstinence from meat. That is how the tradition of eating fish on Fridays arose. Medieval scholars went so far as to suggest that duck should be regarded as fish and not meat on the grounds that ducks swim in water!

The point about fasting is not that it is a duty so much as a voluntary abstinence or denial of that which we enjoy precisely so that we can enjoy and appreciate God's provision all the more. It also indicates to us who really is in charge of our bodily wants. Is it our own self or do our desires rule over us? Surrendering these desires to God restores a healthy balance in our life. Fasting can help us to identify with those who have no choice but to go without. It reminds us of our frailty and our humanity. Fasting also allows us to use the time that we save (either by fasting from food or television or some other time-consuming activity) so that we might redeem the time and use it for prayer.

13. 'Wasting time'

Some years ago I went on a guided retreat. At the time I was wrestling with some significant life questions concerning my future direction and I wanted to see some development of my spiritual life. I went to see my spiritual director for the week, expecting to be given some challenging meditative tasks and deep issues to consider. Instead, he suggested I weed the garden and chop firewood. I imagined that he hadn't really understood my situation or that this was just for the first day. It turned out that these tasks were all I did for the whole week and it was a very restorative time. The retreat centre didn't particularly need these tasks doing and in some ways they were pointless tasks, but what it did for me was to relax me and get me back in touch with myself. We can take ourselves too seriously at times and pottering is a wonderful antidote.

14. Keeping a journal

Some like to keep a journal for every day of their life and use it as a deliberate and methodical way to keep track of the issues that are in process for them. However, that is not the only way to use a journal. It is also valuable to keep a journal during particular times of intense reflection and engagement. For example, it is useful to use a journal during times of retreat or for particular periods of reflection. The forty days of Lent could be one of those times. The value of a journal is to use it to see how particular issues are progressing over time. It can be a great encouragement to look back and see how some questions are resolved over time.

15. Personal review
Reflection is a structured way of reviewing our life and work. There are various models that one can use to structure reflection. A common model is that of the river. Imagine the various stages of a river, the babbling brook, the fast flowing stream, the larger river, the river in flood, the river near the estuary – wide and slow, the river as it reaches the sea and comes to the conclusion of its journey and purpose. You can place the various events of your life at these points on the journey of the river. Where are you now and what seems to be important for you now?

16. Retreat
A retreat is a longer time of being apart with God. It can be as short as a day or as long as a month. Typically retreats are several days long and usually need to be at least that long to allow enough time to unwind and relax. Those who run retreats report that many who come on retreat seem to spend large portions of the first day asleep! Once we get beyond weariness we are in a better position to be able to listen carefully to what God has to say to us.

Monasteries and retreat houses that offer the possibility of sharing in the regular offices of the day are helpful in that they provide a structure for the day. It is possible to be alone together. In other words, we can have the benefit of the company of others at worship and meals but still have large portions of time when we are alone with God. One does not have to use such places but if you have another favourite location it will be important to create a structure to give some shape to your time away. You might want to set an objective for your time away and then use a journal to check how that objective was met.

17. Discernment
There are moments or periods in our lives when we feel we are at a crossroads or a time of decision. Perhaps we have

been offered a new opportunity which needs to be explored or we may be experiencing conflict or unease. Rather than making decisions under pressure it can be valuable to put time aside – it may only be half a day – and consciously list the advantages and disadvantages of the choices we might make. We can then place these advantages and disadvantages before God and ask for his guiding discernment.

18. Deeper thought

From time to time we might take the opportunity to study a particular subject in depth and to use that study to reflect on our own walk with God. For example, we might choose a topic such as fasting, or types of prayer, or even some passages of Scripture that are difficult. As we engage our minds in learning new insights we can also offer these insights to God in order to ask the question, what can we learn about our own life from these insights. How are we being transformed by God in our ordinary, everyday living?

19. Relaxation

Play or relaxation has a valuable role in helping us to recover our equilibrium. All too often leadership is sufficiently demanding that we don't make enough time for play. It is important to be able to find refreshment in some activities that we enjoy, even if it might appear to us that we are wasting time that we don't really have. The inability to make regular time for recreation indicates that we have a lack of balance in our lives. While it is understandable for us to go through periods where rest and relaxation is difficult, that should not continue for too long a period. We might ask ourselves, if we did have time in abundance, what would we do that we would really enjoy? Is it possible to ensure that we do include some playtime in our lives on a regular basis?

20. Submission
Life in the monastery is a life of submission. One of the problems for church leaders is that the more able a leader is the less likely he or she might be to accept submission to another. Why should one submit to others when it is obvious that you are competent? Creating structures that enable others to express their view and being willing to have others do things in a way that you might not is a conscious discipline. We are not called to 'Lord it over others' as Jesus pointed out so clearly to his disciples. You might want to ask yourself how often you are submissive. One of the advantages of a led retreat is that it often requires a conscious act of submission to the suggestions or even the directives of the retreat leader.

21. Service
Following on from the willingness to be submissive is the regular practice of service to others. Busy leaders look to delegate tasks and that is undoubtedly wise but if it leads to a situation where the leader never gets their hands dirty in the ordinary and mundane acts of service then delegation can be unhealthy. As a mark of humility and a sign that he served the people, the medieval monarch of England washed the feet of the poor every Maundy Thursday. The poor of a particular parish were chosen and to remind the monarch that service grows greater with time, the custom was to wash the feet of the same number of poor as the age of the monarch. Over time, it was thought undignified for the monarch to actually wash feet and money was substituted instead. Even today the tradition of the monarch distributing the specially minted Maundy money continues but the value of the original symbolism has been lost along the way. Are there opportunities to 'wash the feet' of others that you can make part of your regular routine?

22. Daily routine

By definition, most of life is unremarkable, it is not the mountain-top experience. Indeed, if that were not so then mountain-top experiences would lose their value. But it is not true that God is only present in the remarkable, even if it would seem easier to see him acting in these out-of-the-ordinary situations. A useful discipline can be to take time to see God in the ordinary. How do we do that? Perhaps we can set aside a day that is likely to be ordinary, routine and potentially unremarkable and set ourselves the discipline of looking for the activity of God in the regular round of life. What is God saying and doing through others that we meet? How are circumstances ordered such that we can become aware of God being present? Where do we see God's provision? What can we give thanks for in the ordinary events of the day? Developing a thankful and observant heart can help to make us sensitive to the leading of God in the everyday.

As we remarked at the beginning of this list, this is not intended as an exhaustive list and you may be able to add other disciplines to these but hopefully these areas will provoke your imagination. Remember that the goal is to sensitize us to the will of God, to remind us of his love for us, to encourage us to seek his purpose for our life and to be obedient to that. We are called to joy and we can often see that joy in the extent to which we have fun, generate friendships and engage in rest.

Notes
1. Pat Keiffert of Church Innovations, St Paul, Minnesota, gave this information to the author in a private conversation in Vancouver, Canada, June 2005.
2. The issue of spiritual warfare is a vast subject in itself. Together in Mission has a teaching unit on this topic as part of a course on Missional Leadership. The author who developed this topic, Paul Miller, has written an extensive study comparing the approaches of

Walter Wink and Peter Wagner on this matter. See also Mitchell, Roger and Ellis, Roger, *Radical Church Planting*, Crossway Books, 1992, pp. 109ff.
3. Foster, Richard, *Money, Sex and Power: The Challenge of the Disciplined Life*, Hodder and Stoughton, 1985, p. 1.
4. This list is drawn extensively from material produced by Roy Searle for a training course produced by Together in Mission. Some of this material will be published by Roy in a book due to be released in 2006.

Chapter Eight
Churches that Plant Churches

David Garrison, in a remarkable book called *Church Planting Movements*,[1] describes the emergence of church planting movements in a number of parts of the world. In an effort to give a flavour of his subject, Garrison contrasts church planting movements with a number of related movements which overlap what he is describing. First he says that church planting movements are not the same thing as people movements. He defines people movements as those times when significant numbers of people, usually in a particular ethnic group, see large numbers of conversions in a relatively short period of time. He points out that these are usually strongly evangelistic in tone and do not always result in new believers gathering in churches. Where this does not happen the converts usually fade away and there is no long-lasting fruit. It takes church planting to cause people movements to have long-lasting significance.

Garrison goes on to say that church planting movements are not the same thing as the Church Growth Movement – a movement that began through the teaching of Donald McGavran at Fuller Theological Seminary, Pasadena, California. He characterizes the Church Growth Movement as associating 'bigger churches with better churches'[2] and goes on to claim that Church Growth thinking tends to concentrate on responsive harvest fields, advocating that resources are concentrated in these areas alone. I would take issue with Garrison that this was McGavran's original thinking although I take the point that this is what Church Growth teaching has become in some Western settings. Garrison suggests that church planting movements have originated in some very unlikely settings among people groups that many would have seen as unresponsive. He notes that church planting movements are associated with the principle that smaller is better.

I would want to add to Garrison's analysis that church planting movements are not the same thing as the Cell Church movement. Although it is true that Cell Churches emphasize that which is small, they are usually the instrument of a larger church unit. To date, Cell Church movements have originated in parts of the world where there is already a high degree of responsiveness to the gospel and arguably represent an imaginative means of both coping with growth and with accelerating growth. The jury is still out as to whether and how Cell Church activity can produce evangelistic growth in parts of the world where there is not a ready receptivity to the gospel.

By indicating what a church planting movement is not, Garrison is beginning to suggest what it is. He suggests that 'Church Planting Movements are simply a way that God is drawing massive numbers of lost persons into saving community with himself'.[3] Crucially, these movements have usually not originated in the Western world but have grown in parts of the world where one might not have expected dramatic growth to have taken place.

Garrison offers five characteristics of a Church Planting Movement. First, he claims that these movements reproduce churches rapidly. What does he mean by rapidly? While Garrison does not immediately make this clear apart from indicating 'faster than you might think', he offers the fascinating criteria that it would mean starting churches sufficiently fast that the rate of church planting will be faster than the population growth. The point he is making is that church planting movements are going to impact a given ethnic group such that Christianity becomes either a majority of the population or at least a very substantial and influential minority. The idea at least is to reach the whole population within a few generations.

Second, church planting movements are in the business of multiplication. In order to achieve the kind of growth that can reach whole populations, it is necessary to think of multiplication and not just addition. In this framework, churches plant churches at an impressive rate. That kind of multiplication requires that a new church will be thinking of another plant within a year or two. The original mother church will not be content with just one daughter church but will continue to plant year after year. Because the churches that are being planted are themselves planting churches the net result is exponential growth. Another way of describing that growth is to say it is growth that is out of control. In other words, it is not the result of a plan or even a set of goals, it is simply spontaneous, organic growth.

Third, church planting movements are indigenous in nature. For any movement to be a movement it must be led by leaders from the people group in question. That does not mean that cross-cultural missionaries are not present at the inception of the movement but it does mean that they are able to develop significant local, indigenous people quickly. Non-nationals can remain present but they must move to a support role quickly. New converts must have the feeling that this new movement is culturally recognizable and not an import.

Fourth, church planting movements take responsibility to plant churches. Garrison is simply making the point that in the first instance, the early plants might be planted by missionaries but within a very short period of time the primary responsibility for reproduction lies with the indigenous churches. Movement begins when non-nationals cease to take responsibility for new plants and responsibility shifts to nationals.

Fifth, church planting movements operate within people groups or interrelated people groups. The initial impulse of rapid church planting occurs within homogeneous people groups. As these movements take root, the power of their conviction causes them to want to reach other groups that are not radically different from the original group but are slightly different in some respects. In other words, these movements are transferable to related groups provided that the boundaries are not too great.

Garrison goes on to document a number of church planting movements around the world. None of these are in Western nations. Despite this absence of evidence in Garrison's work, is it then possible to see any evidence of church planting movements in the West? There is little doubt that the vigour of movements in the developing world is overspilling in many Western nations where migration is bringing significant numbers of people to the West.

In terms of sheer numbers, the impact of migration is probably most significant for the United States and it would not be an overstatement to say that what happens in the religious story of migrants to the USA will shape the future of Christianity in that land. At this moment in time there is evidence of rapidly growing church planting movements. I have met some of these church planters. They come from Haiti, Brazil, Ethiopia, Columbia, Mexico, Nigeria and the Dominican Republic to name but a few.

Those who are planting are extraordinary people. Often they support themselves in a secular job, send money to extended families back home, attempt to get an education and then plant a church as well. I have met church planters who are car mechanics, yellow cab drivers, carpenters, shoeshine boys and labourers. Their hard work, faith, commitment and sheer exuberance is infectious. Church leaders that have spotted the potential for church planting among ethnic groups and are willing to take indigenous leadership seriously are already seeing a significant difference in the overall growth of their denominations.

In Europe, migration is also impacting church life in many European cities, nowhere more so than in the City of London. It is claimed that today more than half of all worshippers in inner London are drawn from ethnic minorities. Of the four largest churches in London, all of them many thousands strong, three are heavily dominated by minorities from overseas, whether from South America, West Africa or even South Africa as thousands of white South Africans come to live in the Greater London area. Churches from denominations that are new to the shores of Europe are springing up in church halls, schools and meeting rooms of every description.

One researcher has attempted to track the number of new churches in a single London borough, Newham, and has identified dozens of congregations that do not seem to appear on anyone's radar screen. As with many movements, keeping an accurate track of what is happening is very difficult. It is all too often the case that an understanding of what is taking place doesn't receive much attention in the studies of sociologists until the wave of growth has fully matured.[4]

Perhaps one of the most remarkable of these overflowing movements from the developing world is that of the Redeemed Christian Church of God, founded in Nigeria in 1952. The story of this church is recorded in outline in the book *Out of Africa*.[5] It is worth taking some time to gain a flavour of the growth of this church in order to grasp something of the spiritual dynamic overflowing from the developing world.

The Redeemed Christian Church of God was started by Josiah Adindayomi who had become a Christian in 1927 through the work of the Church Missionary Society.

Although unable to read or write, Josiah had received a vision of strange symbols on a wall.

> He was instructed to copy down what he saw, which he painstakingly copied onto a wooden board. He took the board with him to the home of some of his relatives in Lagos who read out the name: Redeemed Christian Church of God. On hearing that this was the name the Lord has instructed him to give the church, his family mocked and derided him. Undaunted, he further disclosed that in the vision, God had told him that this church would spread to the ends of the earth and would still be serving faithfully when the Lord returned to the earth in the Second Coming.[6]

The young church grew strongly in Nigeria and came to a critical moment when the founder died in 1980. His successor, Enoch Adeboye, was a very different personality. He had been a Professor of Mathematics at Lagos University and brought a change of direction to the young church. As he explains in *Out of Africa*, on becoming leader he saw the need to cast a new vision:

> The following became the vision statement for the RCCG:
>
> - To make it to heaven
> - To take as many people to heaven as possible
> - To make holiness our lifestyle
> - To plant a church of the RCCG within five minutes of every home worldwide.[7]

The change of leadership marked a distinct shift of emphasis within the denomination. There was a conscious attempt to reach middle-class professional people and that enabled the church to connect with Nigerian professionals who had migrated to other nations. In 2004, it was estimated that the RCCG had 6,000 churches (or parishes as they call them), in 50 different nations. In the United

States in that year there were more than 150 parishes with their annual convention attracting some 7,000 participants.[8]

In the United Kingdom there were more than 120 parishes in 2004 and church planting continues at a rapid pace. Within Nigeria the RCCG is well known for its annual Holy Ghost Congress which began in 1998. It is hard to know how many attend but crowds have been estimated in excess of 6 million people. In London, large all-night prayer meetings are held in major stadiums with as many as 20,000 people in attendance.

The rapid growth of this single denomination illustrates the extent to which church planting movements are beginning to be witnessed in the West, beginning from vigorous movements located in other continents. That then raises the question, if church planting movements need to become indigenous, are there any signs of indigenous church planting movements beginning in the West?

That is a very difficult question to answer. As we suggested in chapter two, some research suggests that there could be the beginnings of rapid church planting movements which some call 'simple church'. We will explore this phenomenon in more detail in the next chapter. For the moment we can certainly say that there are thousands of people meeting in small groups in homes in a number of Western nations and that this could amount to an incipient movement.

At this time the jury is out and the reason for caution is that it is hard to know how many of those who are meeting in home groups have simply dropped out of church and how many are meeting in the kind of groups that are not only multiplying rapidly but are reaching mainly new converts as a consequence of their multiplication. We cannot yet know if that is taking place. However, it is worth asking the question, what would encourage such a movement? What ingredients need to be present in order for a church planting movement to flourish?

In the book, *Invading Secular Space*, I suggest that movements have four distinct phases.[9] First, the Divine Spark, the initiation of movement that really does belong with God. I also suggest that there are more of these 'Divine Sparks' than we sometimes suppose and that in one sense movement is always a possibility. Second, an Interpretative Framework. By this I mean people on hand who can explain the message of a movement in terms that address the fundamental life concerns of those who are being reached. Third, the Multiplication of Many by which I mean structures that are sufficiently transportable and replicable that ordinary people can multiply the impact of the original experience without experts being required. Genuine movement is always lay-led. Fourth, Power, Permanence and Purpose, which requires the creation of sufficient structure that the movement is adequately resourced, intellectually, spiritually, and in terms of abilities and gifts. Structures that serve movements are always necessary and only become a problem when the movement is asked to serve the structure.

Beyond these observations, are there things that we can do that would make the generation of movement more likely or are we merely helpless, simply waiting without influence on our world for something to turn up? It is my conviction that God does prompt us to act and that in a critical sense the future is never closed. God is a God of hope and even though the church does sometimes go through periods when we seem to need to breathe in rather than breathe out, to be refreshed in order to be released, we should never think that dramatic change is out of the question. I am always reminded by a study of church history that most of the astonishing times of expansion in the life of the church took place at times and in situations when nobody was expecting such a thing to happen.

In a classic study on the nature of mass movements, still in print since 1951, Eric Hoffer offers some valuable pointers in relation to the generation of movement.[10] It should be noted that Hoffer was writing just after the Second World War and he had in mind not just religious movements but political mass movements too. Naturally he was somewhat suspicious of movements, seeing in them the capacity to do great harm as well as much good. In some ways that makes his study all the more penetrating.

Hoffer suggests that all movements require propitious times. For Hoffer, movements only begin when there is a feeling of dissatisfaction. It does not have to be a sense of injustice or oppression nor even the presence of grinding poverty, though these would also create the conditions for a movement. He suggests that there simply has to be a sense that something is wrong, that society in some important respects is coming unglued.

Are we living in such times? Caution is called for. It is no surprise that there is spiritual dynamism among immigrant communities, partly because of the spiritual fervour in their own homelands and partly because immigrants are precisely the groups that Hoffer suggests are always receptive to movements of hope. But what about the indigenous populations of the West? Certainly, if you talk to Christians you quickly catch the sense that they see cultural, social and spiritual decline in the West. If the media are to be believed, Pope Benedict also has a strong sense that Western Europe, and to some extent the wider West, is in serious cultural and spiritual decline and has set his agenda accordingly. But not all feel as we do. It is certainly possible to speak to many young people who feel that these are wonderful times of freedom and opportunity.

Yet the balance might be shifting. It does not require everyone to feel that something is amiss in order to see the conditions to encourage movements to develop. There are some early indications that the coming generation of those who are now in their mid-teens are beginning to yearn for different values. They seem to be socially more conservative and yet in terms of a willingness to be involved in social action, are radical in their thinking. Pope Benedict has suggested that young people in Western Europe are under-challenged. If he has read the situation aright and if those same young people are ready to be challenged the conditions for movement may be emerging.

In her book *The New Faithful*, with the intriguing subtitle *Why Young Adults are Embracing Christian Orthodoxy*, Colleen Carroll attempts to document a shift in spiritual attitudes among the youth of America.[11] She freely acknowledges that the evidence that she is looking for is ambiguous. There seem to be numerous shifts in attitudes that are operating simultaneously. Some of those shifts are taking significant numbers of young people towards a more serious search for Christian faith while at the same time other young people are drifting away from religious faith. In the midst of this conflicting evidence, Mark Driscoll strikes what seems to me to be a realistic tone.

> In Seattle, the young men are, generally, pathetic. They are unlikely to go to church, get married, have children, or do much of anything else that smacks of being responsible. But they are known to be highly skilled at smoking pot, masturbating, playing video games, playing air guitar, freeloading, and having sex with their insignificant others ...
>
> ... While the rest of the organizations in the city are busy trying to clean up the messes made by these young men, including unwed mothers, fatherless children, and crime, we focus our efforts on converting them and training them in what it means to be a godly man. So far our training on everything from how to study the Bible, get a job, invest money, buy a home, court a woman, brew beer, have good sex and be a pastor-dad to their children has been very successful for hundreds of young men.[12]

That seems to me to suggest that the conditions for a movement are potentially present, but movements don't begin without some specific intervention – in fact precisely the kind of intervention that Mark Driscoll's church is attempting. That brings us to the second of Hoffer's observations. Movements require leaders of a particular kind.

First, leaders of movements inculcate audacious dreams. It is not a case of any dream will do – the more preposterous the better. The dreams that such leaders begin to articulate do sound far-fetched or at least very ambitious at first. Listening to the accounts of the leaders of movements, you hear again and again of how those who are still with them on the journey had difficulty taking them seriously at the beginning – the vision sounded too big. In every case, the vision came to these leaders out of a growing conviction that such a dream was coming to them from God and could be realized for that reason.

We are not describing ranting demagogues – often these leaders are quietly spoken, but also quietly convinced. It is not that God will do everything, they can see their part, but they are confident that God will open doors and go ahead of them. How do leaders manage to gradually convince others that this vision is possible? Two factors seem to be present. First, their characters inspire confidence. They are honest, trustworthy people whose lives to date convey authenticity. Second, even though they have a larger dream in mind, they also have some shorter-term activities which are also worth achieving. Most of those who join them on the journey can at least be convinced that the smaller, short-term objectives could be achieved. Belief about the larger aims could be suspended while the shorter-term activities were attempted. As these smaller projects come to fruition it lays the ground for the next, slightly more ambitious project to be attempted.

Second, the leaders of movements know how to take action. The leaders of movements are not merely dreamers. Often they have been successful in other spheres of activity before sensing the call of God for a particular task. They have an ability to see what can be done. They are able to take action as well as dream dreams. Hoffer comments:

> Men of thought seldom work well together, whereas between men of action there is usually an easy camaraderie. Teamwork is rare in intellectual or artistic undertakings, but common and almost indispensable among men of action. The cry 'Go to, let us build a city, and a tower' is always a call for united action.[13]

One of the most encouraging aspects of church life in the last few years has been the extent to which Christian leaders have been willing to come together across denominational divides to consider what can be done by churches together within communities, across towns, cities and even regions.

These co-operative efforts have often begun around prayer. While prayer is always intrinsically valuable, where prayer has been the sole ingredient, the activity tends to die out after a short period of time. The bonds of co-operation only extend to a certain number of prayer meetings! However, on occasion there have emerged some leaders who have seen the potential for action beyond the initial dynamism of prayer. Often they have been prompted by prayer to conduct research into the needs of the communities they are praying for. In part the research is intended to direct prayer more effectively but intuitively it also lays the foundation for further action. Good research that identifies needs and issues leads then to action. That action, together with the process of prayer and reflection supported by research, often leads to the galvanization of a vision for the area in which they are working.

My observation is that even these three activities are not sufficient to actually implement a vision. There also have to be present leaders who are committed to detailed planning and to the massive mobilization of leaders supported by local leadership development that also requires significant training processes. The leaders of movements are sufficiently committed to the vision that they are willing to get to this level of practical action to see the vision enfleshed on the ground.

But it is not just a matter of knowing how to take action. Somewhere along the line, leaders of movements have taken a decision to act. For them, it is not enough to see that something could happen or even to hope that it will. They have a determination that something will take place even if they don't immediately know how it will happen. The decision to act begins to occupy their waking thoughts, their night-time dreams, their imagination, their faith, their expectation and their prayer. They are moved to call others together, to look for those who will be enthused by a call to the same end, those who can also see the possibilities and who are only looking for someone to give a lead. Deciding to engage in church planting, the very decision itself, causes a leader to reassess the resources that they have, the content of their ministry, to be looking for others to share in this journey and to see where the opportunities might lie in order to make the venture a reality. This level of committed action implies one further mark of a leader of movements.[14]

Third, they have the capacity to surround themselves with able lieutenants. We could go further and say that insecure leaders either rid themselves of those who are able or alternatively they fail to retain or recruit others with ability. By contrast, the able leader is sufficiently confident in their own ability and in God that they always seek to recruit the most able people that they can find. The building of a team is essential. No leader can accomplish a vision through loyal foot soldiers alone. Dietrich Bonhoeffer uses a striking phrase in one of his books. He says, 'God hates visionary dreaming.'[15] By this he means that there is a dangerous tendency for individuals to take their desires and force them onto others, believing their vision is from God. Those who are the authentic Christian leaders of movements have an openness to the vision that God is painting that allows others to contribute to the painting.

Fourth, no matter how gifted the leader, movements generally require a period of incubation before they grow dramatically. In situations where leadership is inexperienced or where resources are lacking or when there is not a high level of receptivity to the message, the incubation phase can occupy a significant length of time, on occasion as much as a couple of decades. What transpires in the incubation period? This is when the culture of the movement is established, the team is built, and trust established. It is also a period of experimentation when the incipient movement attempts a whole variety of initiatives some of which will work and some of which will prove to be a disaster. It is not that no progress is made in the incubation period, but the progress is not nearly as important as the lessons learnt.

I am convinced that there are sufficient gifted leaders within the churches of the West that the generation of church planting movements, and indeed related movements of other kinds, is entirely possible. There are enough grounds for believing that there is some receptivity to the gospel, certainly more than existed thirty or forty years ago, to believe that there is an opportunity to begin some remarkable movements in the Western world. The conditions for movement may not be perfect but then they never are.

How then should this discussion of church planting movements impact the humble church planter? One church planter who I know well, having planted his first church reflected on the experience and said, 'I don't know if I can do that again.' It had not been a bad experience but it had been a surprise as to just how much effort had been required. Now that he was in his middle years, he began to see that if he did do the same thing again he might only ever plant one more church in his lifetime. As he reflected on what his hopes had been for life he realized that he had hoped that he would have achieved more than planting two churches in his lifetime. He has determined that if he ever plants a church again, it will be a church that plants churches that can plant churches. In other words he wants to help inculcate a church planting movement and not just be a church planter.

If every church planter could be making a contribution to the creation of a church planting movement rather than simply planting a church we might yet be able to write the story of the re-evangelization of the West. It is therefore vital for church planters to pay attention to what they are planting and to ensure that there is sufficient missional DNA combined with an expectation of movement that every church plant is a contributor to movement and not just a consequence of method.

In practical terms that means thinking through the processes of replication at every level of church life. Every time we establish a small group structure, or a youth programme or some community outreach we need to be thinking how we can ensure that there is a process of replication. We need to create structures such that new leaders will emerge to multiply all that we are doing and carry it over into the next expression of church that will emerge from this congregation in the foreseeable future.

Notes
1. Garrison, David, Church Planting Movements: How God is Redeeming a Lost World, WIGTake Resources, 2004. and a booklet with the same name, Church Planting Movements, IMB, Southern Baptist Convention, 1999.
2. Ibid (book), p. 24.
3. Ibid (book), p. 27.
4. Marchant, Colin, Smith, Greg and Sagheer, Mohammed, Mapping Religious Organisations in the Inner City: The East London Atlas of Faiths Project, Given at Religion and Locality Conference at the University of Leeds, September, 1998 and available from the web on

mysite.wanadoo-members.co.uk/credoconsultancy/leedspaperme-thodatlasoffaithgregsmith.pdf
5. Wagner C. Peter and Thompson, Joseph, *Out of Africa: How the Spiritual Explosion Among Nigerians is Impacting the World*, Regal Books, 2004.
6. Ibid, p. 206f.
7. Ibid, p.
8. Ibid, p
9. Robinson, Martin, *Invading Secular Space*, Monarch, 2003, p 196f
10. Hoffer, Eric, *The True Believer: Thoughts on the Nature of Mass Movements*, Perennial, 1951.
11. Carroll, Colleen, *The New Faithful: Why Young Adults are Embracing Christian Orthodoxy*, Loyola Press, 2002
12. Driscoll, Mark, *The Radical Reformission: Reaching Out Without Selling Out*, Zondervan, 2004, p. 184.
13. Hoffer, Eric, *The True Believer: Thoughts on the Nature of Mass Movements*, Perennial, 1951, p. 121.
14. Ibid., p. 114f.
15. Bonhoeffer, Dietrich, *Life Together*, SCM, 1954, p 16.

Chapter Nine
Simple Church

Church planting needs to be understood primarily as a mechanism that contains the potential to engineer to people movements. In this chapter we will explore the potential relationship between saturation church planting and people movements. The term 'simple church' has been coined by Tony and Felicity Dale to describe a phenomenon that looks like the creation of a series of home churches but which contains a capacity to multiply into a movement. We could argue that simple church as a descriptor applies only to a particular form of church that is functioning in the West but which gained its inspiration from movements that originated in the developing world. A few illustrations from the developing world will help to convey the flavour of what we are describing.

David Garrison describes a number of these movements in his booklet entitled *Church Planting Movements*.[1] He describes one movement among the Bholdari people, a people group of some 90 million people based largely in four Indian states and living in more than 170,000 villages. Although Christianity had been present among these peoples since the nineteenth century, the churches that had been established were very few in number and worse still had experienced a long decline in the latter part of the twentieth century. That decline had been sufficiently serious that by the late 1980s, none of these churches had managed to reproduce themselves for a period of twenty-five years.

A fresh start was attempted in 1989 when the Southern Baptists sent a strategy co-ordinator to work with these people. After a difficult and almost disastrous start, an approach was refined by 1992 that centred on locating a 'man of peace' in villages where it was hoped a new church might be started. Garrison continues:

> In 1993, the number of churches grew from 28 to 36. The following year saw 42 more churches started. A training centre ensured that there would be a continuing stream of evangelist/church planters spreading the word. Along the way, churches began multiplying themselves. In 1996, the number of churches climbed to 547, then 1,200 in 1997. By 1998 there were 2,000 churches among the Bholdari. In seven years more than 55,000 Bholdari came to faith in Jesus Christ.[2]

A second illustration is drawn from an area of China which Garrison calls for reasons of diplomacy, Yanyin. In a culturally diverse area of around 7 million people consisting of five different people groups, another strategy co-ordinator located just three local house churches comprising eighty-five believers all of whom were Han Chinese. The believers were mostly elderly and their churches were declining. Employing a similar approach to that used among the Bholdari people, a new movement developed. Garrison describes the results.

> Aware of the enormous cultural and linguistic barriers that separated him from the people of Yanyin, the missionary began mobilizing Chinese Christian co-labourers from across Asia. Then, partnering these ethnic Chinese church planters with a small team of local believers, the group planted six new churches in 1994. The following year, 17 more were begun. The next year 50 more were started. By 1997, just three years after starting, the number of churches

had risen to 195 and had spread throughout the region, taking root in each of the five people groups.

At this point the movement was spreading so rapidly that the strategy co-ordinator felt he could safely exit the work without diminishing its momentum. The next year, in his absence, the movement nearly tripled as the total number of churches grew to 550 with more than 55,000 believers.[3]

A third example is taken from the Khmer people in Cambodia. The Protestant church had been present in Cambodia since the early years of the twentieth century but had always been small, numbering no more than 5,000 believers before the arrival in power of the Pol Pot regime. By the time of Pol Pot's explusion from power, only 600 Protestant believers could be identified. Another strategy co-ordinator from the Southern Baptist association attempted an indigenous church planting strategy. This approach had a wider significance than the movement among Baptists. According to Garrison, Christians in Cambodia credit this initiative with turning the tide so that from 1990 to 1999, the number of Christians in the land had grown from 600 to 60,000.

Garrison describes the work of the strategy co-ordinator as follows:

> Instead of planting a church himself, as had previously been his custom, the missionary began a mentoring relationship with a Cambodian layman. Within a year, he had drawn six Cambodian church planters into his mentoring circle. Over the next few months, he developed a church-planting manual in the Khmer language and taught the Khmer church planters doctrine, evangelism and church-planting skills using resources such as the JESUS film, chronological Bible storying and simple house church development. He also instilled in them a vision and passion for reaching their entire country with a Church Planting Movement.
>
> In 1993, the number of Baptist churches grew from six

to ten. The following year, the number doubled to 20. In 1995, when the number of churches reached 43, the Cambodian church leaders formed an association of like-minded churches which they called the Khmer Baptist Convention (subsequently changed to the Cambodian Baptist Convention)... By the spring of 1999, Baptists counted more than 200 churches and 10,000 members.[4]

These case histories are by no means unique and could easily be supplemented from other stories in the developing world. It has often been our custom in the West to listen to these stories and suggest that what is happening in the developing world cannot be replicated in the West. There are certainly some issues that we need to consider carefully before we unquestioningly attempt to replicate models from other parts of the world, but perhaps we have not learnt as much as we might.

Tony and Felicity Dale, an English couple who have lived for a significant period of their lives in the USA, had had sufficient contact with overseas examples of the rapid growth of simple home church planting movements to wonder what could happen if some of the same principles were utilized in the post-Christendom West. Working in Austin, Texas, the Dales have begun a process of establishing small home churches in a network across the city. The principle involves encouraging believers, preferably relatively new believers, to locate 'people of peace' in their neighbourhoods, work places, schools or other social settings and establish home churches that are very simple in structure.[5] They utilize interactive Bible studies, encourage prayer and very simple forms of worship. The structures require no paid pastor, no buildings other than those like homes that exist for other purposes, no worship band and no professional expertise.

The Dales report a very high level of growth through first-time converts as well as having the capacity to reach those who would have considered themselves well outside of existing Christian churches, structures and influence.[6] Flowing from this activity has come a wider association with similar groups, in the USA and in other Western nations. A publication and a website service encourage the growth of this developing movement. At this early stage, the Dales are understandably reluctant to talk about numbers but sufficient progress has been made to suggest that models drawn from the developing world do have a significance and a relevance for the Western world which needs to be explored.

Before we do that, there are a number of issues arising from the experience of the Dales that require some further questioning and comment.

Issue One – Is it possible to gather home groups together for celebratory worship? When listening to the Dales and more especially to those who would see themselves in the position of learning from the Dales, it can sound as if there is a dogmatic opposition to the creation of any meeting which cannot be contained in a home. That runs counter to what is actually happening in many of the developing world's church planting movements. It doesn't take much arithmetic to work out that 'home meetings' are often fifty or more people. It may be that some in the 'simple church' movement have misheard the Dales or it may also be that they have inadvertently picked up something of that same aversion to meetings other than what happens in the home church from writers such as Wolfgang Simpson.[7]

One of the consequences of this impression is that the leaders of existing churches can feel unduly criticized. It can sound as if the exponents of 'simple church' are saying that anything that meets in a building cannot possibly be a missional church and that God has no further use for the existing church. The inference can be that existing churches should sell all their buildings and head for home church. The feeling that there is a clarion call to Christians to 'come out from among them' could be seen as heralding the arrival of yet another New Church movement with all of the division and bad feeling that took place alongside the undoubted good fruit.

That is to misunderstand what is at stake. The Dales are certainly not encouraging existing churches to move out and sell up. What they are saying though is that there are some issues that those of us in the existing churches need to think through if we want to engender the development of movement. The first of these is the fact that our existing structures do tend to 'lock up' significant quantities of gifts and abilities in the many members who in effect become spectators in our pews. Granted that many of those who have spectator status live busy lives and are actually looking for a place of rest that demands little, you still can't build movements that way.

Second, even though Christendom in a formal sense may be dead, it still occupies our imagination in terms of a default model of what church actually looks like. At an early stage in their development of home churches, the Dales called groups together for larger scale celebration meetings. They would now say that they did this too early. The net effect was to convey the message that it was this larger gathering that was really the church and that the home groups were actually elements, or cells, in the true church – the large gathering. That was not what the Dales were intending to convey because to do so tended to remove the sense of autonomy and hence responsibility for their own life from the home churches and transfer it to whoever led the larger gathering. Shifting the sense of where responsibility for life and so reproduction lay tended to slow down the element of movement.

Third, the point about the home church is not that it meets in a home, there is nothing of a doctrinal nature about the locus of a home because a simple church could equally well meet in another setting, it is more an issue of resource and hence speed of replication. Homes already exist and cost nothing to rent. Simple structures do not need finance for salaries or time to put a leader through seminary. It is therefore much more likely that simple structures will multiply rapidly. That is not to say that larger gatherings and indeed purpose-built buildings cannot follow movement, but they cannot drive it and must not hinder it.[8] It also needs to be noted that there are examples of movements that have been given some buildings that previously belonged to smaller churches, who recognized that they were unable to provide them with a viable future and wanted a Christian future in those buildings more than the money that a sale would have provided. Using these well-located, existing buildings that came at no cost has not hampered the development of movement.

Issue Two – Are there particular people groups in the West that simple church might work with best? I would like to suggest that there are particular groups in the West for whom simple church is highly significant as a point of entry in the creation of a movement. I want to identify at least three people groups.

First, young adults and youth. In the United Kingdom, less than 1 per cent of young adults and youth currently connect with any form of the church. The same would be true for most European nations. I remember hearing the account of a Christian friend of mine (who is in his early twenties) of a visit to Belgium. He had been in Belgium on business for a short time and during this visit had come to know colleagues of a similar age in a social context outside of work. The reaction to his Christian faith was a degree of incredulity rather than hostility. 'But church is only for older people' seemed to be the general response. Relying on the sometimes quoted idea that young people will somehow 'get religion' as they get older and wise up is an ill-founded notion.[9] We need to take some strategic initiatives with those under thirty years of age not unlike those among the Khmers and Bholdaris.

We are talking about significant numbers of people. In the UK in very approximate terms, there are 3.5 million people in each generational group within a five-year age range. Therefore, in the UK alone there are 14 million people aged 10–30, the overwhelming majority of whom are unreached and yet spiritually open. The value of a simple church approach to this group is that it offers them the possibility of leadership and responsibility from the very beginning.

Second, there is an argument to suggest that those who are older than thirty and have no significant contact with the church to date represent a people group all of their own. Their culture, beliefs, hopes and expectations need to be researched and culturally relevant ways of reaching them identified. The work of Philip Richter and Leslie Francis, cited in *Mission-shaped Church*, suggests a helpful way of thinking about the spiritual commitment of the UK population. They identify 10 per cent as 'regular' church attenders and 10 per cent as fringe. Most of our existing evangelistic efforts go into reaching the 10 per cent fringe and trying to rearrange the 10 per cent regulars from one church commitment to another.

Richter and Francis categorize 20 per cent as closed dechurched and 20 per cent as open dechurched. By this they mean that the open dechurched could be won back to the church with creative and sensitive approaches. That leaves the fascinating figure of 40 per cent unchurched. This group mostly has a neutral attitude to the Christian message and is certainly not hostile. My suggestion is that this group in particular could be reached with a simple church approach to mass movement. Again the home church approach allows new converts to quickly take responsibility and leadership so that rapid growth can take place.

Third, those from migrant communities who have a faith background other than Christianity. Let's imagine what could happen if those who are second-generation migrants from a Hindu, Sikh, Buddhist or Muslim background organized themselves around the kind of home church movement that has occurred in the developing world. The huge advantage of small groups is that they are not provocatively present and noticeable in a physical sense. They could happen in sympathetic homes but they can also function in cafés or college campuses or in sports centres. There is every indication of both openness and identity turmoil in these groups that cause them to be very open to a simple church approach.

Issue Three – the DNA matters more than the form. There is nothing special about meeting in a home. Many church plants that have later become fairly traditional church plants have begun in homes. It is perfectly possible to adopt the form of simple church but still fail to see rapid multiplication. What matters is the missional life of the group. This is not a matter of developing a checklist of ingredients. Garrison supplies his checklist of the ingredients that tends to push a simple house church structure towards the development of rapid multiplication and we will return to that list later. Again, it would be possible to find house churches that seem to have all of the elements on the list and yet still do not manage to produce the life that causes these elements to have movement significance.

What is it then that sparks potential life into actual life? My hypothesis is that the answer lies in what we have called previously apostolic leadership. I don't mean to suggest that each house church will have an apostolic leader. These kinds of leaders are sufficiently unusual that we cannot expect to see an abundance of apostolic types. But somewhere in the early modelling we should expect to see an apostolic figure who generates the initial spark and whose leadership manages to infuse the wider home group structure. In terms of Garrison's analysis, the apostolic person is not the strategy co-ordinator that he describes but rather, someone or some people in the initial indigenous group of leaders that the strategy co-ordinator has worked with. In one or more of these people must lie an apostolic gifting if movement is to take off.

Having suggested that apostolic types are not available in vast numbers, I also want to suggest that they are not so rare that they hardly exist at all. My suggestion is that apostles are more common than we might think and that part of our activity must be to help locate these individuals in parallel with the kind of activity that helps to inculcate missional DNA. It might actually be the case that the careful nurturing of a healthy DNA pool might actually assist in the emergence of apostolic gifts. What kind of missional DNA are we trying to encourage?

Garrison lists ten universal elements which he indicates are always present in church planting movements. Some of these, for example prayer and the acceptance of scriptural authority, are the kind of elements that we would expect to be present and so I do not propose to comment on these. Underlying some of the other elements, there seems to me to be a recurring theme that is not often discussed. What this amounts to is a degree of intentionality in the activity that gives rise to a heightened sense of expectation as to what might occur. It is in this heady brew that some exceptional leaders seem to emerge.

There are at least three ways in which the theme of intentionality arises. First, the expectation that new churches will be planted and they will be planted rapidly. Garrison suggests that beginning with this goal in mind impacts what is likely to be produced. At a very basic level, if the intention of leaders is to produce a movement of praying people then praying people is what tends to emerge from such an intentional activity. If the intention of a group of people is to make Scripture widely available then Scripture distribution programmes is what tends to eventuate.

Garrison is making the point that leaders do not commonly begin their prayer, planning, envisioning and strategic creativity with the assumption that large numbers of churches can be developed and developed quickly. There may be good reasons for leaders not beginning with this set of expectations. It is possible that their experience of church planting is that it is hard work, slow work and resource hungry. That experience will shape their future expectations such that the intention to plant churches on a significant and rapid scale just does not enter the equation. Garrison suggests that it is time to look at church planting movements elsewhere and reposition our imagination and expectations.

Second, Garrison is claiming that rapid multiplication only occurs when it is accompanied by abundant gospel sowing. The more that we position our members to share their witness widely the more likely it is that evangelistic fruit will follow. Simple structures such as home church ensure that leaders are kept close to the ground. They do not lose the network of connections that they have in the community because they become too busy maintaining a complex organizational structure. Keeping those potential evangelistic contacts is vital because it enables a continued gospel sowing.

We need to remember that lack of response to the gospel does not necessarily indicate a lack of receptivity to the gospel so much as the reality that the gospel is not shared very frequently either through personal testimony or through mass media in many Western contexts. Garrison particularly makes the telling point that many church planting movements have begun in situations that were not initially receptive to the gospel. Receptivity grew in direct relationship to the number of times that personal witness was made.

Those of us living in the West might want to look at these kinds of claims with a degree of incredulity. Surely, we might say, Garrison doesn't understand that the reason we have stopped sharing the gospel message is that we have been discouraged by the results when we have shared it. More of the same, we might protest, will not necessarily bring success. But perhaps our protestations do need to be reviewed. There is some evidence that whenever there has been significant sharing of the gospel, positive results have followed.

Let me offer two illustrations. First, the widespread use of the Alpha course in Western contexts has revealed that there can come a significant response to the gospel. The difficulties experienced with the Alpha course have not so much been obtaining positive responses but rather that invitations to non-Christians have sometimes been thin on the ground because our existing membership seems to have few relationships with those who might be invited. Moreover, in some situations where invitations did result in good attendance and in a high response rate, there has come difficulty incorporating converts into what already exists. This is not a sign that there is poor receptivity to the gospel so much as we have problems within the life of the church that need to be addressed.

The second illustration flows from a number of situations that I know personally where ministries in schools have demonstrated that there is receptivity among significant portions of young people. Once again the problem lies not in receptivity but in what to do with young converts following their commitment to Christ. Assimilation into existing church structures remains a significant barrier.

Third, Garrison calls for the use of lay leadership on a huge scale. Moreover, he suggests that converts be mobilized in terms of the dream even before they have fully made commitments. That is not to say that there should be no trained leadership but only that the initiative should lie with lay people. It is almost certainly the case that the best leaders that any church planting movement will have are yet to be converted.

It follows that the overwhelming majority of leaders will be lay and not professional. Some of these lay people will receive some practical training on the job, some may also receive some payment but they will largely remain bi-vocational. It was this model of very local leadership that powered the huge church planting movements that took place among nonconformist churches in the emerging cities of nineteenth-century Britain and on the expanding frontier of nineteenth-century America. Indeed, some have argued that growth only stopped once the professional clergy finally got control of these runaway movements. We need to learn from our own Western history as well as from movements in the developing world.

These three requirements, to expect and strategize for rapid multiplication, to engage in massive gospel sowing and to keep lay leaders at the forefront of movement means that the structures we operate must be capable of replication. In short, the front line of the advance must be composed of simple structures because only simple structures can enable these requirements to stay in place. Simple church therefore means in the first place replicable church. The main issue is not that that the church must meet in a home; it is only that a home church contains the possibility of ease of replication. As we indicated earlier in this chapter, merely because a group meets in a home does not mean it will replicate.

It is at this point that we face a common problem with Western thinking. All too often we have become obsessed with a model, believing that the selection of the correct model will lead to the right results. It hardly matters whether we are talking about emerging church models, fresh expressions of church or even simple church, it is all too easy for the advocates of new models to view the model itself as the critical issue. I want to suggest that our tendency to want to find a successful model and replicate the model rather than the missional activity that lies underneath has led to a whole succession of difficulties ranging from experimentation with Willow Creek style churches, Purpose Driven churches, Cell Church, G12 and many others. Good models develop from good missional practice much more than the other way round.

That is not to say we should have no interest in experimental models, whether simple church or any other. Nor is it a case of any model will do. Rather, the test becomes, can the model permit and encourage the missional behaviour that we have outlined above? This remains a critical issue because in truth there have been numerous outbreaks of movements in the West that could have become people movements had they not been choked off before wider movement could develop.

I know of at least two movements in UK senior schools that impacted a very high percentage of pupils over a three to five-year period. I know of at least five local churches in the UK that saw significant numbers of converts from particular people groups in their community. Over the last twenty years, dozens of church leaders have told me of times when they saw remarkable moves of God that lasted for a short time and then stopped.

As I have listened to these various accounts and revisited in my own mind the situations that I have personally witnessed, I want to suggest that what occurred in these situations was the following. First, the horizon of expectation was limited. In the case of the schools, the leaders were simply amazed at what had happened and their priority was to pastor the converts and establish them in local churches. Their horizon was not, how can we expand this movement to every school in our region? Second, no replicable structures were generated. The leadership remained with those whose priority was to pastor converts. Imagine what could have happened if leadership had quickly passed to the converts. Third, converts were steered into existing church structures that did not have the capacity to foster movement only to absorb and tame it. That taming of movement was not intentional but it was the inevitable result of a lack of experience in terms of people movements.

Because God is God and because people are always asking spiritual questions, even if they do not know that is what they are asking, people movements are always a possibility if we are able to work with the energy that emerges. None of these comments are designed to criticize or belittle the work of church leaders in the West – I am one of them and know only too well the confidence-sapping, exhausting experience of Christian leadership in the West over these last few decades. However, I am beginning to wonder if the arrival in the West of dynamic movements of God from other parts of the world might be God's signal that it is time to think fresh thoughts, to regain confidence and to dare to believe that great things might yet happen in the lands in which we labour.

Notes

1. Garrison, David, *Church Planting Movements*, International Mission Board of the Southern Baptist Convention, 1999.
2. Ibid., p. 23.
3. Ibid., p. 17.
4. Ibid., p. 28.
5. Dale, Tony and Felicity, *Simply Church*, Karis Publishing, 2002, pp. 103ff.
6. Information gleaned from a conversation with the Dales in my home in July 2005.
7. Wolfgang Simpson has written extensively on this subject see particularly his book *Houses that Change the World* which is a private publication and can be downloaded from the web.
8. See McGavran, Donald, Understanding Church Growth, Eerdmans, 1970 comments on the creation of people movements, see especially chapter 17, pp. 221ff.
9. See account in Kimball, Dan, The Emerging Church: Vintage Christianity for New Generation, Zondervan, 2003 and Cray, Graham, Mission-shaped Church, Church House Publishing, 2004, p. 40 f.

Chapter Ten
Going Public

Exponents of models such as 'simple church' call into question the need for any kind of public building. At a deeper level they are asking a question about the whole relationship of the church to the public square. The intrinsic though not explicit answer to the question, 'How does the church influence society or the world?' is that the church will do so through individual witness. It thus holds fast to a perceived pre-Christendom model of individual influence through the personal honesty and integrity of each believer. If enough individuals are Christians then surely we will have a Christian society.

There are at least three objections to such a view of the relationship between church and world. First, many look at nations such as Rwanda and Northern Ireland where personal piety runs high and Christian influence on the underlying power structures of the land has been very weak indeed to the ultimate shame of the church and discrediting of the gospel. Second, there is evidence from the pre-Constantinian church that Christians did engage in social action and where possible did meet in public meeting places.

Third, it views the early church through an Enlightenment lens. The idea of the importance of the individual is a modern phenomenon. It is almost certainly the case that early Christians saw themselves in terms of communities. It was the corporate witness of the community and its relationship with society that mattered and not just that of the individual Christian.[1] These are complex questions that will need to be debated elsewhere, but the church planter needs to face some immediate practical issues in relation to buildings and the relationship of the new congregation to its immediate context.

As we have seen from our discussion on movements, the issue of buildings can be a thorny question for church planters. It is an issue in terms of both principle and practice. Let's take a few moments to examine the question of principle. For the moment, we will remove the issue of practice by suggesting that a church planting team has been offered the gift of a new building in the area in which they want to plant with no cost to the ongoing work other than its maintenance. They quickly realize that the maintenance costs will be less than the rental they were going to pay for a local school on Sundays and offices midweek. Although this is a hypothetical situation, I do know of some church plants in the UK that have been presented with precisely this dilemma.

At one level it is a no-brainer. Surely the church should take the building, save the money and be grateful for such an encouraging beginning? It might even be interpreted as a sign of God's provision. However, there are at least two problems attached to such an acceptance. First, the building defines the vision. In some of the cases that I know, where a building was offered, its provision left the church with problems of size in relation to their vision. The building could only hold around 120 people and the vision of the church planters was for a much larger church. Admittedly they could have held multiple services but that would have meant beginning with multiple services – not an easy way to start! In other ways too, for example the lack of auxiliary rooms, this was not the building that the new church would have built if they had been doing the design work. A well-intentioned gift quickly became something of a millstone.

Second, the building helps to express the culture of a church. In one case that I know, a developing church plant was offered a building which was superb in that it was just the right size, it had adequate auxiliary rooms and in terms of facility was just what the leaders of a developing church would have wanted. Its location was ideal and again it came entirely free. But the style of the building – unmistakenly a church and nothing else – was not very helpful in expressing what this developing church was trying to say about the nature of the church and of worship. The building was at odds with the worship style that they were reaching for. Even though they were starting afresh it felt as it they were doing battle with the tradition of the ages.

What we have said so far suggests that if a new church plant is to have its own building then at the very least, the design and provision of a building should not be entered into with undue haste. The developing plant needs time before the planters are ready even to imagine what kind of building they require. But we need to ask a more difficult question than that. There are some who take the view that the very ownership of a building used for public worship ties a church to a hopelessly outdated Christendom model of church. Should newly emerging churches ever, as a matter of principle, own their own building? Before we come to a view on this issue, we need to consider two difficult issues for any church wishing to connect with the mission field in the West.

The first relates to the question of sacred space. Whatever our building solution, we need to take seriously the ways in which those we are trying to reach respond to sacred space. The spontaneous life of a small group that is part of a movement creates its own sacred space through prayer, worship and the perceived presence of God. That dynamic is precious but is not easily transferred to the larger worship setting. As we leave modernity behind which tended to demean sign, symbol and sacrament, we are likely to find that these elements of spiritual expression will again become important for believers and seekers alike. Generating a sense of the transcendent presence of God in a school hall takes a certain amount of imagination.

Western culture is slowly beginning a search for the holy, a reality that is evidenced by the increasing growth of attendance at worship in many of the great cathedrals of England. A friend, who had recently preached at St Paul's Cathedral in London, told me that he had two congregations in the same service. One congregation, large in number and attentive, sat in the chairs provided. A second congregation, curious and reticent, stood behind the pillars, somewhat in the shadows. Sacred space draws these anonymous seekers but it is also an important element in the development of a community seeking to follow God.

The second issue concerns the question of permanence. Whether we like it or not, for those that we are trying to reach, the presence of a church building sends a signal about our determination to stay, to be present for the long term. That is not in itself a reason to build but it does raise the serious question as to how long one can continue to meet in homes or in rented buildings or some combination of the two. One church I know, with a congregation close to 800 if all were in attendance, has met in a school hall, among other buildings, for some twenty years.

It would not be difficult to imagine the church in question still meeting in that same school hall for another ten years at least. But the tensions that a lack of permanent space have generated have been considerable. The question 'Can we find a place to build or buy?' has been on and off the agenda for many years. In part it has been resolved by purchasing substantial offices with some small meeting rooms and a large meeting room that could seat around 150 people. The church does not meet there on Sundays, but at least in the summer it could easily do so and sometimes does. It is hard to avoid the growing demand for a building.

So why not build? The reality is that the issue, to build or not to build is not fundamentally an issue of principle but one of practicality. Church buildings are expensive to build and expensive to maintain. There is little question that to build or purchase a building too soon in the church planting exercise can seriously slow any movement that you have worked so hard to engender. Not only so, but the very act of owning a building can easily distract the attention of the church in such a way that the building becomes the mission. There would be few in the church that would put it that way but in reality, when an analysis is undertaken of the expenditure of money, time and activity, there is little doubt that buildings easily move from the position of servant to master.

That should cause us to think, not should we own a building but rather, if we did, how would it serve the mission and therefore what would it look like and what functions would it serve? It may be that we are in the same position that the medieval church was in when it had to think seriously about the question of buildings. Prior to that, the Celts had a simple system – as the church grew they didn't provide any buildings for public celebration, only prayer cells.[2] As congregations grew, worship had to be outdoors. In the northern hemisphere that no-nonsense approach to physical comfort has its problems and so at some point the emergence of buildings was almost inevitable. The first buildings in that period tended to be wooden because people also lived in wooden homes, but as stone replaced wood the church faced a dilemma. Then, as now, it seemed to be asking a great deal to have the largest, most expensive building in a community used for only a few hours in the week.

The medieval answer was to ensure that it wasn't only

Going Public 177

used on Sunday's or indeed only for worship. The medieval solution was to separate the holy part of the church, the chancel (previously the chapel and earlier the prayer cell), from the main body of the church, the nave, with a screen called the rood screen. The secular business of the day was conducted in the nave, with the chancel and the high alter well screened off. Churches were used for markets, debates, concerts and community meetings of many kinds. Sacred space and secular space lived cheek by jowl, so much so that in later times, some reformers complained about dogs wandering into the church and urinating on the alter. That was too close a connection with everyday life for some!

It may be time for the church to rethink the nature of the buildings that we use for worship. The question we must ask is not whether the church should own or alternatively operate a building but how it can be used, and how does that use relate to the issues of mission and finance? One church I know, in the United States, bought an existing factory for their intended church plant. Half the building was remodelled as a church and the other half remained as a factory. There is a clear glass wall between church and factory reminding those in church of the world outside in a very graphic fashion. In the half that has been remodelled to hold Sunday worship, there is extensive space for adult education classes and training of various kinds. Between the factory and the training function, the building pays its way leaving the finances of the church free for mission.

Whatever solution to its potential building needs that a particular church considers, it is important to remember that every building sends a signal to potential attendees long before they come inside the building. Does the building look inviting or intimidating? Can it even be seen from the roadside? Have we thought through our signage so that the entrance is obvious? Is there ease of car parking for those who will need it? Have the needs of the disabled been built into the facility or is provision an awkward afterthought? Remember that schools do not always convey a positive message for those who did not enjoy their school experience and who might even have been bullied at school. Consider carefully the messages that your chosen physical solution to your building needs sends to those you wish to reach, whether you own it or rent it.

It is time to reimagine the kinds of partnerships that we might enter with local government, business, community groups and schools to see how the resources that the church does have in terms of volunteers and a certain amount of finance for rental or its equivalent, can be used creatively to benefit the community. That imagining does not need to be entered into hastily or under pressure. It is almost always better to take time to develop a church plant in small groups, in community enterprise and service and in building as many relationships as possible before making a commitment to a regular public worship service.

The launch date

Let's conjecture that a particular church plant was going to use the model of developing evangelistic and discipling home groups before a public launch. How much time should one allow, for example, between the gathering of an initial home group and the decision to hold a regular public worship event? The answer to that conundrum is not so much related to time as to activity. There are certain realities on the ground that it is advisable to have in place before a public launch. First, as we indicated in chapter three, it is advisable to have at least fifty and preferably more people in small groups before a launch.

Second, you need to be sure that you have the significant resources of musicians, preachers, worship leaders and set-up teams before launch. Remember that once you are using these people in this way then that could prevent them from being as involved in their present ministries.

Third, it will be important to ensure that you have sufficient home group leaders to cope with a sudden influx of those who want to join the church either as mature Christians or as those who require discipleship. In conjunction with that assessment, you need to ask how you will handle those who want to join the church as mature Christians and whose value system turns out to be diametrically different to the values of the developing church. Have you some kind of new membership class in place that can address those kinds of questions?

Fourth, significant connections will have been built with the community either through schools, community associations, neighbourhood groups or indeed any local expression of community that you can find. Through these connections, the community will have become convinced of the positive value of your network of Christians and may even begin calling you a church before you have planned your first worship service. Your goal is to create a climate of welcome such that the launch of a new church is not perceived to be a hostile act, the arrival of a strange sect or generally a problem that the community could do without. Creating that climate of welcome will include building strong relationships with the existing churches such that their perception becomes one of welcoming fresh workers to the field rather than fearing the arrival of competition.

In any event, it is vital not to rush into a public launch too quickly. That kind of public statement represents a landmark both in the life of a church and in your relationship with the community. You will need to get it right because to misfire on this occasion is to lose your greatest single opportunity to move beyond the networks that you have already generated and to connect with many new people in a short period of time. That is why you must be sure you are ready for such a development.

The reality is that it is all too easy to get a public launch wrong and that once we have launched we are somewhat stuck with the constant weekly effort to ensure that the public face of the church goes well. This reality has led some to ask whether any kind of public celebration is actually necessary. Is it not possible for a network of home groups to continue to expand almost as an underground movement? Before we move too dogmatically in such a direction, we might ask ourselves why it is that those movements that have been forced by persecution to operate in cell groups and which have seen significant growth under those circumstances, have always opted to hold public celebrations on a significant scale once persecution has been removed. It would also be instructive to ask whether those acts of going public with celebration have caused those movements to cease to grow.

This is not the place to engage in an in-depth investigation of that issue, although it would surely be a fertile research area for someone, but even a cursory examination of recent events in China and Ethiopia would suggest that it is by no means inevitable that the growth of cell groups is terminated by the lifting of persecution and the arrival of public celebration. I want to suggest that the critical issue in determining whether growth can continue or not lies in the relationship between cell group leadership and the leadership of the celebration event. As long as the culture of the broader group is driven by the priority of developing leadership at the cell group level then continued growth is likely. Growth is only choked off if the coming of public worship somehow undermines the cell group leadership. Worse still, if public celebratory worship places all leadership in the hands of a professional class of clergy such that all other leadership is devalued and no longer developed, then movement ceases immediately. In some situations where such a development did take place but dynamic life was still around, the result has often been to produce a schism with new organizations emerging to retain the previous lay-led structures.

Creating the climate for church planting

So far, we have focussed on what a single church plant might do in order to encourage a warm climate of acceptance for their public launch. But are there steps that the wider Christian community might take in order to produce a generally positive climate for church planting? It is sometimes very hard for Christians to assess exactly how they are perceived by society more widely. The signals can be confusing.

On one occasion I was speaking to an American minister who has been working in Australia for some time. He was generally enjoying the experience but he did remark on the extent to which clergy seemed to have little or no social standing in Australia as compared with the United States. My friend felt that it was by no means automatic that a clergyperson would be regarded as a community leader simply because they were ordained. The right to be seen as a community leader has to be earned. Indeed, he went further and suggested that all too often clergy were seen negatively either as potential child abusers or as charlatans or as socially reactive. They certainly were not seen as imaginative leaders constructing a better future for the community.

Probably many Christian leaders have felt this negative press and it is often enhanced by the very aggressive stance that some media seem to take with regard to the church. Just recently I read a British newspaper article that was giving a Christian charity a rather negative review. Rather than noting that this was a charity that worked with the poor, they accused the charity somewhat harshly of 'targeting the poor'. It was a curious choice of words. I am not sure what else a charity that worked on behalf of the poor would do other than target the poor but the words were deliberately chosen as an accusation of wrongdoing.

Again, I have just finished listening to a report from the BBC World Service giving a negative spin to the growth of the church in Cambodia. The line that the reporter was taking was that the growth of the church was a bad thing because it was undermining local culture. In reality the growth of the church is taking place through the enterprise of Cambodian Christians who are taking their own culture very seriously. It is partly for this reason that the church is growing. The BBC reporter commented on how sad it was that the worship of trees, stones and local gods was being wiped out by the growth of Christianity. It takes the genius of the BBC to turn a good news story about Christianity into bad news.

But we should not think that media hostility tells the whole story. There are also signals in Western culture that point in a very different direction. Just under 72 per cent of Britons described themselves as Christians in the last national census.[4] For most people, including Christian leaders, that finding was something of a surprise. (It was difficult to present this figure negatively but one news report did try with the comment that 'only' 72 per cent of the British population are now Christian.)

In my local community in a suburb of Birmingham, England, an annual inter-church carol service held in the open air regularly attracts around 5,000 people who view it as the only way to start Christmas in that part of Birmingham. A team, planting a church in an English suburb, consulted with the community before taking a final decision to plant. The overwhelming opinion in the community was that a church would be a good thing. Many expressed the view that the opening of a church would make this new housing area a genuine community.

It is easy to be cynical about those positive signals as representing the last remnants of a dead and dying Christendom. But that would be a superficial reading. The truth is that bringing the gospel to Western ears is both harder than we might like to think but more possible than we sometimes imagine. The future is genuinely open and there is a great deal we can do in the public square to tip the balance.

On a broader campus, it is certainly possible for the Christian church to engage positively with the worlds of politics, education, arts and the media to begin to present a positive view of the Bible, Christianity and the Church. We can learn from those in the past, for example the Clapham Sect, who did so much to shift secular opinion in the late eighteenth century towards a positive evaluation of the Christian faith. It is also sensible to learn from the positive community involvement of the church in much of the developing world. This kind of broader involvement that applies the Christian faith in the public square is one factor in helping to produce a positive environment for receptivity to the gospel.[5]

There are many positive indications that Christians are taking seriously the call to influence society at this macro level.[6] These developments can have a symbiotic relationship with church planting. The more effective Christians are in developing a positive profile for Christianity, the more that church planting will be well received and indeed welcomed. The more that church planters exercise imagination and creativity in developing healthy expressions of the church on the ground the more credibility there will be for attempts to influence society more widely.

As a strategic approach to mission in the West develops, leaders in the wider church need to pay attention to three critical areas in relation to church planting. First, we need to call together those who have a strategic desire to reach immigrant communities to consider how we might be able to create movements within those communities. It is no good lamenting that some of these communities are difficult to reach with the gospel. We could learn something from the Nigerian churches as they have sought to be strategic in winning the Muslim north of Nigeria to Christ. If you want an example of a really difficult task then that would be it. The church planting agenda of the Nigerian church in the North is an object lesson in what can take place.[7]

Second, we need to pay attention to cities. In many important respects, cities drive Western culture in terms of its future direction. Even if the church in the West significantly strengthened its presence in the suburbs, if we miss what is taking place in our cities we are likely to be sidelined in terms of our culture. Nowhere is this more true than in cities like London with their strong influence on media. Ironically, we are stronger in major cities than we sometimes think because of the growth of the African and South American populations. But the historic churches are poorly informed about this development, they often do not see its significance and rarely have church planting strategies even though they could easily recruit workers from those same communities if they attempted it.

Third, we need to have strategies for whole communities whether they are cities that include suburbs, or towns, or villages and sometimes strategies for whole regions. As we saw in an earlier chapter, there are some indications that these strategies are emerging at a grass roots level.[8] It has been fascinating to note how often it has been lay people that have been at the centre of some of these developments. In at least three cases that I know of in England, the leaders have been medics, two of them having returned from overseas missionary service as medical doctors. We now have enough experience of these inter-church strategic models that we are probably in a position to fan the flame to bring many more models into being. The positive witness that flows from Christians obviously working together is significant for the unchurched and particularly for civic leaders.

Fourth, we do still need denominational strategies for church planting. Increasingly, in the Western world, Protestant denominations are adopting church planting strategies, but the denominations or networks that actually have such policies and place significant resources of recruitment, finance and training behind them are still a minority. Many denominations are still only planting sufficient new congregations to cope with the replacement of closures, and most are not even doing that. Denominational church planting needs to have considerably more energy injected into it.

Planting and the wider task of mission

Let us remind ourselves that the act of church planting is not an end in itself, it represents one element in a broader engagement with Western culture. The intention of church planting is to produce missional congregations. The act of planting significant numbers of mission-shaped churches should help to leverage change in existing congregations. That does raise the question as to whether it is possible to bring change to existing church life. Can existing churches become part of a single movement that has the intention to re-evangelize the West or are existing churches merely that which is to be replaced by the new forms of church yet to emerge? There are certainly some who doubt that the revitalization of that which exists is possible at all.

It is likely that your answer to that question is as much a matter of personal temperament as it is a matter of objective measurement. Speaking as one who has attempted the renewal of existing congregations, I am very aware that the renewal of that which exists is even harder work than church planting and that it takes longer than it does to church plant. Moreover, the evidence that emerges from those who have successfully transitioned existing churches to something that resembles a missional mode is that the systems and tools required to bring such a thing about are sophisticated and complex to operate. It takes determination, consistency and a long-term involvement to pull it off.

That kind of commitment has to be a call in just the way that church planting is a call.

It has to be hoped that we can call into being sufficient men and women who are committed to church planting in addition to significant numbers of leaders who are committed to processes of revitalization. We are all headed in the same direction, namely the re-evangelization of the West. As we consider the awesome size of the task, we need to remind ourselves that the task is sufficiently large and difficult that it will require a dedicated commitment from large numbers of people. Some have spoken of the extent of that commitment as the need for a new monasticism.

That theme has been emerging from some very diverse quarters and some unexpected sources. Four brief examples make the point. The present Pope Benedict is said to have chosen his name precisely because he sees the need for a new monasticism that will produce the willing and disciplined workers to renew Europe (and the West) at a time of cultural decay. Those who have written of the work of Taizé have also remarked on how the founder, Brother Roger, was inspired by the writings of Bonhoeffer on community. Using those writings as a foundational source, the monks at Taizé have also been attempting to forge a new kind of monasticism in Europe, always looking to the young to bring hope and renewal.

The Northumbria Community, with its mother house at Hetton Hall in Northumbria, has sought inspiration from the Celtic saints, so important in the bringing of Christianity to Northumbria in particular but more widely to the Europe of the Dark Ages.[9] They have attempted to found a dispersed missional order, ecumenical in commitment, that is centred on the spirituality of the Celts but also takes seriously the mission that Celtic spirituality was intended to promote. The Anglican-Baptist church of St Thomas located in Crookes, Sheffield, has for some years been host to Bob and Mary Hopkins and their ministry

Anglican Church Planting Initiatives. In order to help encourage more church planters into the field, they have recently begun a training mechanism which they call The Order of Mission or TOM for ease of communication. The order has been recognized within Anglican structures.[10] These four examples of approaches to a new monasticism are by no means the only responses and it is very likely that yet more will be founded in the coming years.

But why a new monasticism, why not just more workers for the field? In one sense it is simply a case of more workers, but the significance of the imagery of the monastery is twofold. First, we should remember that the original monks, whether Benedictine or Celtic, were often the church planters that participated in an amazing reconversion of Europe. The popular imagination sometimes associates monastic orders only with being shut away from the world. In reality, much of Europe was reached with the gospel by church planting monks. Think of the first missionaries in England during the Dark Ages. In the south of England, Augustine arrived in AD 604 and established the first mission in Canterbury. He was a Benedictine monk and so were his fellow missionaries. The first Celtic missionaries arrived at Lindisfarne in AD 632. These first preachers of the gospel were all monks and they quickly established church planting activities as the gospel spread.

Second, those that we require on the contemporary mission field of the West need to be workers of a particular kind, in the sense that they have seen the reality that the cultural crisis of the West demands more than just effective evangelism. We are calling people to a new way of life which, as we explored in an earlier chapter, is at heart counter cultural. To establish functioning communities that are in the world but not of the world requires a body of disciplined people. Whether we call them monks or not, whether we see them as a formal order or not, the disciplines of a monastic order will be necessary if new spiritual communities are not to be drowned in the easy hedonism of a very material, and on its own terms, very successful culture.

That reminder of the need for spiritual life underlines the reality that the re-evangelization of the West will not be quick and it will not be easy, but it is possible. The church needs workers who are ready for the long haul of mission and not the quick fix of the latest methodology. Ultimately the responsibility for success lies with God. He has graciously called us, may we graciously serve.

Notes
1. See Kreider, Alan, *The Change of Conversion and the Origin of Christendom*, Trinity Press, 1999, for a wider discussion of the nature of the early church as community and the relationship of social action to evangelism. See also a discussion on similar topics in See Robinson, Martin and Smith, Dwight, *Invading Secular Space*, Monarch, 2003, pp. 59ff.
2. Robinson, Martin, *Rediscovering the Celts: The True Witness from Western Shores*, HarperCollins, 2000.
3. See the earlier discussion in relation to the launch number of 50, p. 69f.
4. The religious question was added to the most recent census after a successful campaign by church leaders. The initial difficulty was that the civil servants with whom the discussion was held were genuinely puzzled as to why anyone might want such information.
5. This point is part of a much wider argument about the way in which Christianity engages with the public square. See Robinson, Martin and Smith, Dwight, *Invading Secular Space*, Monarch, 2003, pp. 59ff.
6. To learn more of the work of Artisan consult the web on www.artisaninitiatives.org
7. Wagner C. Peter and Thompson, Joseph, *Out of Africa: How the Spiritual Explosion Among Nigerians is Impacting the World*, Regal Books, 2004, pp. 172ff.
8. For an earlier reference to local coalitions see p. 152f.
9. See again Robinson, Martin, *Rediscovering the Celts: The True Witness from Western Shores*, HarperCollins, 2000.
10. For more information on The Order of Mission consult the web on www.sttoms.net.

Bibliography

Books actually on Church Planting

Conn, Harvie M. (Ed). *Planting and Growing Urban Churches.* Baker Books, Grand Rapids (1997)

Garrison, V. David. *Church Planting Movements.* WIGTake Resources (2004)

Murray, Stuart. *Church Planting, Laying Foundations.* Paternoster Press. (1998)

Christine, Stuart & Robinson, Martin. *Planting Tomorrow's Churches Today, A Comprehensive Handbook.* Monarch Publications (1992)

Stetzer, Ed. *Planting new Churches in a Postmodern Age.* Broadman & Holman Pubishers, Nashville. (2003)

Note: A colleague is known to be producing a book on church planting which is due to be published next year. Title and publisher are not yet fixed, but the author to look out for is Graham Horsley.

Books on Missional Church

Cray, Graham (Ed), Church of England Mission and Public Affairs Council. *Mission-Shaped Church.* Church House Publishing. (2004)

Frost, Michael & Hirsch, Alan. *The Shaping of Things to Come.* Henrickson Publishers Inc. (2003)

Haselmayer, Jerry; McLaren, Brian D. and Sweet, Leonard. *A is for Abduction, The Language of the Emerging Church.* Zondervan, Grand Rapids. (2003)

Hirsch, Alan. *The Forgotten Wave: Reactivating the Missional Church*, Brazos Press (2006)

Kimball, Dan. *The Emerging Church, Vintage Christianity for New Generations.* Zondervan, Grand Rapids. (2003)

McLaren, Brian D. *A Generous Orthodoxy.* Zondervan Grand Rapids, Youth Specialties Books. (2004)

Minatrea, Milfred. *Shaped by God's Heart, The Passion and Practices of Missional Churches.* Jossey-Bass, John Wiley and Sons Inc. (2004)

Books on Cultural Context

Driscoll, Mark. *The Radical Reformission: Reaching Out Without Selling Out.* Zondervan, Grand Rapids (2004)

McLaren, Brian D. *The Church on the Other Side.* Zondervan, Grand Rapids. (1998, 2000)

McLaren, Brian D. *The Last Word and the Word After That.* Jossey-Bass, John Wiley and Sons Inc. (2005)

Murray, Stuart. *Post-Christendom, Church and Mission in a Strange New World.* Paternoster Press. (2004)

Raschke, Carl. *The Next Reformation, Why Evangelicals Must Embrace Postmodernity.* Baker Academic. (2004)